# THE ANALYST'S TORMENT

# THE ANALYST'S TORMENT
## Unbearable Mental States in Countertransference

*Dhwani Shah*

PHOENIX
PUBLISHING HOUSE
*firing the mind*

First published in 2023 by
Phoenix Publishing House Ltd
62 Bucknell Road
Bicester
Oxfordshire OX26 2DS

British Library Cataloguing in Publication Data

A C.I.P. for this book is available from the British Library

ISBN-13: 978-1-912691-84-5

Typeset by Medlar Publishing Solutions Pvt Ltd, India

www.firingthemind.com

Chapter 1, Arrogance, is based on a chapter from a previously published work. Republished with permission of Taylor and Francis (Books) Limited UK, from *Arrogance: Developmental, Cultural, and Clinical Realms*, Akhtar, S. & Smolen, A. G. (Eds.), 2018; permission conveyed through Copyright Clearance Centre, Inc.

Chapter 2, Racism, is derived in part from an article published in *The Psychoanalytic Quarterly*, 89(3) 2020, pp. 399–413, copyright © *The Psychoanalytic Quarterly*, available online: http://www.tandfonline.com/10.1080/00332828.2020.1766935

Chapter 7, Hopelessness, is based on a chapter from a previously published work. Republished with permission of Taylor and Francis (Books) Limited UK, from *Hopelessness: Developmental, Cultural, and Clinical Realms*, Akhtar, S. & O'Neil, M. K. (Eds.), 2015; permission conveyed through Copyright Clearance Centre, Inc.

Chapter 8, Jealousy, is based on a chapter from a previously published work. Republished with permission of Taylor and Francis (Books) Limited UK, from *Jealousy: Developmental, Cultural, and Clinical Realms*, Akhtar, S. & O'Neil, M. K. (Eds.), 2018; permission conveyed through Copyright Clearance Centre, Inc.

*To Mia and Maanav*

*For helping me remember what is important*

# Contents

# Acknowledgments

I would first like to acknowledge and thank my patients, who in our shared experiences gave me an understanding of my limitations and failures which are the basis of these chapters.

This book would not have existed if it was not for Salman Akhtar's warm and generous encouragement to write and reach out to Kate Pearce, an extraordinary editor and human being who has been invaluable in bringing this book to its completed form. Nancy McWilliams and her compassion, vast psychoanalytic knowledge, and editing skills were also invaluable to me and this book exists in large part due to her mentorship and guidance. Travis Smith, one of my oldest friends and an academic I respect and admire, read every chapter of this book and his honest feedback helped me immensely. Andrea Celenza, Kani Illangovan, David Oakley, Rick Salvatore, Jill McGelligott, Holly Haynes, Lisa Rosenthal, Dionne Powell, and John Geller all read many of the chapters in this book and their feedback made this book a much better version of what it was previously. Many of my colleagues in Princeton and at the Princeton University Counseling Center, including Lynn Shell, Loretta Acquaah, Archana Jain, Calvin Chin, Christine Garcia, Jasmine Ueng-McHale, Augusta Tilney, Whitney Ross, Marvin Geller,

Michael Libertazzo, Krista Kalkreuth, Deborah Greenberg, Laura Nash, Antonia Fried, and Laurie Schafer read versions of several chapters in this book and gave honest and thoughtful feedback which was deeply appreciated.

As I describe in the introduction, George Atwood and several other early teachers and mentors in my life influenced me in profound ways and much of their writing style and way of being is in this book. Sylvia Greene was my first real mentor and teacher. She introduced me, as a clueless high school student, to Sophocles, Plato's *Symposium*, Nietzsche, and Sartre and helped guide me to choose the path of learning psychology, religion, literature, and philosophy as an undergraduate. At Rutgers University, James Jones, Bruce Wilshire, George Atwood, and Steven Walker all had a profound effect on me and to this day I remember details of what they taught. They were suspicious of purely rational ways of perceiving the world and were deeply invested in phenomenology, intersubjectivity, and the embodied ways in which we are embedded in the world and with each other. I hope this book carries that tradition forward.

I would also like to thank my wonderful supervisors, mentors, and colleagues at the University of Pennsylvania Department of Psychiatry, the Psychoanalytic Center of Philadelphia, and the psychoanalytic community at large including Harvey Schwartz, Richard Summers, Mark Moore, Barbara Shapiro, Susan Adelman, Sydney Pulver, Michael McCarthy, Sally Holtz, Lawrence Blum, Geoffrey Neimark, Lisa Rosenthal, Ira Brenner, Cabrina Campbell, Johnny O'Reardon, Elna Yadin, Anthony Rostain, Melvin Singer, Marc Lipschutz, Barbara Shapiro, June Greenspan, Deborah Luepnitz, Jacques Barber, Elaine Zickler, Urmi Vaidya-Mathur, Gerald Margolis, Aisha Abbasi, and Barbara Milrod.

Lastly, I would like to thank my parents and sister, Bipin, Ela, and Bindi Shah; Rekha, Rajen, and Shreya Mehta; Deven, Kaya, and Rohan Sukhdeo, and especially my wife Amy Shah and my two children Mia and Maanav for being loving, encouraging, and tolerating me throughout the time I wrote this book.

# About the author

**Dhwani Shah**, MD, is a psychiatrist and psychoanalyst currently practicing in Princeton, NJ. He is a clinical associate faculty member in the Department of Psychiatry at the University of Pennsylvania School of Medicine and a faculty member at the Psychoanalytic Center of Philadelphia. He completed his residency in psychiatry at the University of Pennsylvania School of Medicine where he was chief resident and completed a fellowship in treatment resistant mood disorders at University of Pennsylvania School of Medicine. He is the recipient of several awards, including the University of Pennsylvania PENN Pearls Teaching Award for excellence in clinical medical education, the University of Pennsylvania residency education Psychodynamic Psychotherapy Award, and the Laughlin Merit Award for professional achievement. He has authored articles on topics ranging between neuroscience, mood disorders, and psychoanalysis.

# Introduction

*The capacity for countertransference is a measure of the analyst's ability to analyze.*

—Hans Loewald (1986, pp. 285–286)

There was a time when I thought that my patients lived in a different world than I did. I imagined their world centered upon "character pathology" and "maladaptive defensive coping strategies"; my world involved knowledge and insight, the tools I could use to help my patients get better. I fantasized about taking in everything in the introductory psychoanalytic textbooks on personality psychopathology I treasured—my favorites were Nancy McWilliams's *Psychoanalytic Diagnosis*, Glen Gabbard's *Psychodynamic Psychiatry in Clinical Practice*, and David Shapiro's *Neurotic Styles*—and using the immense accumulated wisdom and insight these authors demonstrated psychoanalysis had to offer. These books had secret knowledge of what was going on inside the minds of my patients, knowledge I could master as a technique to help them.

Of course, this hunger for knowledge had motivations unknown to me at the time. There was an unconscious omnipotent fantasy driving this quest to know—inhabiting the role of "a hero in training," a future champion who could conquer any psychopathology that came my way. The divide between me and my patients gave me a safe distance from their psychic pain to enact this fantasy—clearly, they were the ill ones needing my expert help.

This was also a move away from my own troubled past, my family history, and the ghosts that led me to this strange profession where I am paid to be with mental suffering in all of its forms. Rendering them "the sick patients" and me "the healthy doctor" blocked my ability to authentically know and feel my own personal suffering and to honestly face my patients' inner torment and psychic pain that I could not bear to feel along with them.

I should have known better, if my unconscious did not get in my way. My first psychology professor, who was also the first psychoanalyst I ever came across, was George Atwood. Warm, wise, and self-effacing, George Atwood always emphasized that our psychological theories and formulations about our patients are not objective rational constructs—far from it. They are deeply embedded in our way of being and created by our own subjective experiences, our histories, and the intersubjective space between us and our patients.

In fact, the first psychoanalytic book I was assigned to read as an undergraduate was Atwood and Stolorow's coauthored book *Faces in a Cloud*. Reviewing the lives of several early psychoanalytic pioneers, including Freud, Jung, Reich, and Rank, Atwood and Stolorow demonstrate how their brilliant psychoanalytic theorizing was deeply intertwined with their biographies and life histories. I especially appreciated how Atwood and Stolorow put themselves and their theories on the chopping block as well, describing how their own personal histories brought them to intersubjectivity and self psychology.

This book is an attempt at a similar kind of emotional honesty, although this went unrecognized by me during the process of writing these chapters. In a sense, it is about a shift in emphasis in our psychoanalytic theorizing towards *our* subjectivity, using what we know as psychoanalytic clinicians to understand our own therapeutic motivations, mishaps, and stumbles with our patients. The purpose of this shift in emphasis towards our subjectivity is to highlight what gets in the way of our capacity to face up to what we are feeling and how it is impacting our patients.

George Atwood's emotional honesty and ability to reflect on what was happening within himself in his encounters with patients resonated with me after years of facing my own clinical limitations and failures as a psychotherapist. As Mike Tyson famously quipped, we all have a plan until we are punched in the mouth. Being a therapist requires one to take many punches in often unexpected and painful ways that reach us in our most private and guarded places. To make matters worse, our knowledge of our patients and what they need often ends up being based on our own illusions of healing that can be more narcissistic than helpful. Acknowledging that we never fully know what we or others feel encourages caution, humility, and genuine curiosity about ourselves and others (Jurist, 2018).

One central theme in this book is how our uncomfortable and disowned emotional states of mind are inevitably entangled with our understanding of patients, potentially derailing the therapeutic process as well as at times facilitating it. Our knowledge and formulations of our patients are always inherently flawed and biased, often unknowingly based on our own psychological conflicts.

The chapter on arrogance addresses this potentially problematic use of knowledge directly. Creatively inspired by Bion's celebrated and enigmatic paper "On Arrogance" (1958), this chapter discusses some common ways in which we stop listening and become to varying degrees "self-important, stupid and flat" in the face of uncertainty and intensity. Overcoming our narcissism and being able to be with our patients without resorting to arrogant or masochistic defensive strategies to cope with the unbearable experiences inherent in analytic and psychotherapeutic work is a lifelong struggle for me, and I suspect it is for many of us.

This theme of facing unbearable experiences with our patients is continued in the chapter on racism. Here the focus is on dealing with historical and culturally loaded traumatic experiences outside of the consulting room that collide with associative material in the session, potentially derailing the therapeutic process. I am grateful to Jill McElligott for creating a panel at Division 39 of the American Psychological Association in 2019 on "Clinical Considerations of Psychic Emancipation in a Racialized Society," where I was able to present some of this material with Dionne Powell, a psychoanalyst whose writings and talks on racism inspired much of this chapter.

This focus on what unknowingly gets in our way in helping our patients has echoes of Freud's original ideas on countertransference, which have to do with the unconscious inhibitions and conflicts within us that impede our ability to be an effective analyst. Despite his limitations, there is much to value about Freud's original conceptualizations of countertransference—they aimed to safeguard the patient from the analyst's own unconscious reactions and narcissism that could harm the patient. Returning to Freud's original contributions on analytic listening and countertransference from a contemporary perspective, Pinsky (2017) notes that in stark contrast to recommending treating the patient like a "trite caricature of the silent doctor," with coldness or indifference, ideally the analyst should be "self-restrained and open-minded, non-intrusive and affectively involved," always remembering they are human with limitations (Pinsky, 2017).

Freud originally used the term countertransference to highlight the dangers of analysts' succumbing to erotic transferences. The chapter on erotic dread describes this in more detail and discusses the dreaded erotic intermingling of genders, bodies, and minds that occurs in every in-depth analytic treatment. In contrast to Freud's at times defensively insisting on a need to "conquer" what we are feeling in the erotic countertransference, I highlight contemporary psychoanalytic approaches which emphasize the necessity to be open, curious, and receptive to what is happening within our bodies and our intersubjective self-experiences.

This disruption of our ability to be with our patients in an affective and embodied way is also highlighted in the chapter on dissociation. Our dissociative defenses against psychic trauma and how we create distances between ourselves and our patients by unwittingly removing ourselves from our lived experiences of our body, our affects, and our ability to be present and alive as we encounter and reexperience trauma with our patients is known to all of us but infrequently addressed in detail.

Dissociation allows us to survive our patients' unbearable affects and trauma, but at a cost. I did not understand what this cost was when I first encountered the first psychoanalytic paper that was truly meaningful to me as a psychiatric resident, "Countertransference Hate in the Treatment of Suicidal Patients" by Maltsberger and Buie, written in 1974, published in the *Archives of General Psychiatry*. One of my psychiatric supervisors at the time, an irritable no-nonsense former naval lieutenant who detested psychoanalysis, tossed this wonderful "old school" article at me early in the morning in our psychiatric emergency room after I told him how detached and emotionally exhausted I was by all the trauma and violence I was bearing witness to. "Well, read this and learn about why that is," he growled at me. "If you want to be in this for real you better get used to feeling other people's intensity thrown at you."

This deeply psychoanalytically rich article about our most intense reactions to our patients in crisis, enigmatically given to me by a psychiatrist who had no patience for psychoanalysts, was a revelation to me and, in many ways, another catalyst for this book. Following in the tradition of Winnicott's courageous work, "Hate in the Counter-transference" (1949), Maltsberger and Buie concisely describe why we harbor often unrecognized hatred towards our patients in crisis and how we end up expressing this hatred through various means of aversive tactics, affectively communicating to the patient, "I do not want to be with you." Our patients feel more abandoned in this distanced stance, which worsens the crisis. Allowing space for language that described the emotional onslaught I was facing and how to deal with it clinically helped me immeasurably, and inspiration and direct references to "Hatred in the Countertransference in Suicidal Patients" are featured in several chapters in this book, including the chapters on dread and hopelessness, both of which are unbearable states of mind familiar to all clinicians who work with patients who are suicidal or suffering acute psychic trauma.

The chapter on hopelessness focuses on the collapse of an analytic vision and the often unconscious thwarted *hopeful* fantasies underlying our experience of hopelessness in our therapeutic work. Our often unrecognized dread of our patient's most intense affective experiences and the rupture of empathy that follows from this is the basis of the chapter on dread, which highlights suicidality as an especially potent experience in the countertransference that can stir unbearable feelings that lead us to unconsciously distance ourselves from our patients.

Maltsberger and Buie's article also helped me honestly face up to what they call "the three narcissistic snares" all psychotherapists harbor to some degree: to love all, know all, and heal all. When we inevitably fall short of these ideals, we are prone to experiencing shame, which is an important countertransference experience we all need to face as clinicians. Learning how to face our shame in a dignified way that allows for us to continue to make contact with our patients and grow from the experience is the focus of the chapter on shame, which also describes other difficult and unbearable experiences we shamefully face as therapists, including failure, greed, and envy.

One unbearable emotion I struggled writing about was jealousy. After Salman Akhtar graciously invited me to write a chapter on countertransference jealousy for his edited volume on the topic, I felt at a loss at how to describe this painful and tormenting experience in a clinically meaningful way. Salman Akhtar thankfully introduced me to the writings of Harold Searles and his innocuously titled book *My Work with Borderline Patients* (1986). Searles's chapter entitled "Jealousy Involving an Internal Object" was challenging, shockingly honest, and clinically useful, giving me the inspiration for the chapter on jealousy, included in this book in a slightly revised form.

Harold Searles, Heinrick Racker, Paula Heimann, and other psychoanalytic theorists influenced by Melanie Klein informed my understanding of how my emotional reactions like jealousy can guide me in understanding my patients' inner experience. I have reservations about this way of knowing, as I have outlined in several of the chapters of this book. Overall, however, it is indisputable to me that what we feel, in our affects, bodies, and reveries with our patients, is vital in helping us understand and metabolize their emotional experience. This is fraught and dangerous territory, however, leaving us vulnerable to assumptions, biases, and concrete ways of thinking that can close down the therapeutic process and colonize our patients' minds with our fantasies of what they are going through based on our biased feelings and intuitions.

Being able to first recognize and then make sense of our disturbed state of mind is crucial in these situations. As Busch (2019) notes, it is not just the recognition of a countertransference reaction that is helpful therapeutically for our patients, but this recognition combined with an honest self-analysis of our own contribution. What is essential is the difficult work of discernment, uncomfortable emotional honesty, and sorting out what is happening in every unique encounter within the shared space of both the analyst and patient. We can never assume our feelings are useful or related to our patients' emotional experience without authentically being in the struggle with them. We strive to be responsive, yet disciplined—alert to our internal experience, with the aim of distinguishing between constructive and harmful uses of the countertransference, always with the goal of finding a way to be with our patients (Pinsky, 2017). This type of emotionally honest, uncomfortable, and close attention to the bidirectional and intersubjective processes of what happens between analyst and analysand has its origins in the work of Sàndor Ferenczi. Over ninety years ago, in 1928, Ferenczi wrote that the analyst

> has to let the patient's free associations play upon him, simulta-
> neously he lets his own fantasy get to work with the association
> material; from time to time he compares the new connections
> that arise with earlier results of the analysis; *and not for one*
> *moment must he relax the vigilance and criticism made necessary*
> *by his own subjective trends.* (p. 86, quoted in Meszaros, 2015,
> italics mine)

The variety of ways we fall short of this type of engagement described above is at the heart of what this book is attempting to describe. The focus should always be on the patient and what gets in our way of being able to authentically engage with what is most difficult for them to bear.

This requires the work of mentalization on our part, our capacity to affectively make sense of and interpret behavior in terms of mental states, whether our own or others' (Jurist, 2018). We actively mentalize about our patients' mental states and invite our patients to mentalize about their own mental states and about others', including our own. As Jurist (2018) notes, "All psychotherapy boils down to being a project of two minds engaging each other and trying to make sense together" (p. 2). The process of mentalization is not just about providing intellectual interpretations to patients to further their self knowledge, or to encourage behavioral change. Instead, it is a focus on emotional communication, valuing being able to receive input from others and being vulnerable to revealing oneself to another. Mentalization encourages open-mindedness and "being able to sustain an active, fallible investment in reevaluation of self and others, past and present" (Jurist, 2018, p. 2). This involves the work of improving our skill in identifying, modulating, and expressing emotions. It also requires us to increase our range of emotions we are aware of and being more at ease with the emotional intensity and uncertainty that occurs in our communications with patients.

Our ability to "go there" with our patients and give ourselves over to their unbearable experiences of suffering and annihilating states of mind is in the end what offers the best chance at helping them. As opposed to an overemphasis on focusing on the content of our countertransference reveries to understand our patients, I favor paying close attention to our ability to allow our patients' emotional and subjective reality to impose itself on us, our receptive capacity to be genuinely affected and stay with what is unbearable for them to experience alone (Bollas, 1983; Eshel, 2019).

Here our countertransference reactions can be described as an inability to creatively dream with our patients' emotional life, our ways of avoiding an encounter with the overwhelming pain accompanying their excessive suffering, and the alive, unpredictable, and uncontrollable aspects of the emotional encounter with an other (Bergstein, 2018). By honestly discussing what gets in our way with our patients, we can hopefully find creative and authentic ways of being with their suffering and inner torment that help them have a place to articulate and feel what before was unbearable for them.

### A note about writing about patients

Over the years, I have become increasingly uneasy about writing about patients[1] and clinical material. The intimacy and privacy of a therapeutic setting should be safeguarded at all costs, especially in our current

---

[1] I use the term patient as opposed to "analysand" and "client." My reasons for doing so are largely based in my medical training and feeling comfortable with the term in its associations to a healing profession, despite its potential problematic connotations. The term "client" always felt too business oriented and corporate, and the term analysand, while preferable, is not technically accurate, because some of the patients I describe are in psychoanalytically informed psychotherapy as opposed to psychoanalysis. I interchange the terms "psychoanalyst," "analyst," and psychotherapist as well, in part to highlight how most of what I describe applies to all psychodynamically informed clinicians working with patients intensively. Also, for ease of reading, when nonspecific situations are being referred to, "she" is used for the psychoanalyst and "he" for the patient, but the points raised are applicable to all.

political and cultural climate, where issues of privacy and confidentiality have been shockingly disregarded. The most important virtue a psycho-analytic clinician strives for is confidentiality, because confidentiality is constitutive of the process itself (Lear, 2003).

This book contains numerous anecdotes and clinical vignettes, which constitute a potential breach of confidentiality. I struggled with how to present this material and not compromise my patients' confidentiality and trust. A book intended for clinicians without clinical material seems highly suspect and abstract, especially when it involves our emotional and subjective reactions to our patients and how they affect our clinical treatment of them.

It seems psychoanalytic clinicians who write or talk about patients do so either by getting informed consent from their patients and making minor changes to the clinical material written, or by changing substantial details about patients in order to cover up any relationship to their actual patients in the consulting room. An argument can reasonably be made that the details in a psychoanalytic treatment matter, and without significant details about the patient and the process of what unfolds in the treatment, including various unconscious motivations and meanings, transferences and enactments that occur cannot reliably be made sense of.

Despite this, I lean heavily on the side of preserving patients' confidentiality by fabricating the details in my case descriptions. None of the clinical vignettes in this book are actual patients, they are all imaginary constructions based on my clinical experiences over time and are for illustrative purposes only. In instances when there were details in particular case descriptions I could not avoid, specifically in the chapters on racism, jealousy, and dread, I asked my patients to read what I wrote and was given informed consent to publish the vignettes with any corrections they asked for.

All of them agreed and made some minor changes to what I wrote without protest. Subsequently, a majority of them had associations and dreams of being exploited and misused—as we talked more about it, they all had complex emotional reactions to what I wrote, to my asking them for permission, and to their knowing that it would be published. Of course, I should have expected this, and apparently this is common when permission is asked by the analyst to disclose personal details of a deeply private encounter (McWilliams, personal communication). I also had to face unsettling truths about my own desire to breach the private space of the analytic setting. Alongside a genuine desire to transmit knowledge and expand our understanding of the psychoanalytic process, there was also my desire for recognition as well (Lear, 2003). In the end, I hope I was able to preserve my patients' confidentiality by using case vignettes that are generic and fictional, with the purpose of demonstrating the clinical process and what potentially gets in the way of helping our patients.

# CHAPTER 1

# Arrogance

*Do the cranes crying out in the high clouds think it is all their own music?*

—Mary Oliver, "Her Grave"

The arrogant psychoanalyst is a pervasive stereotype in our culture. "Why are psychoanalysts so damn arrogant?" This question has haunted me in countless ways—at conferences, dinner parties, and casual conversations—even by strangers upon discovering what I do for a living. In an absurd, memorable moment years ago, a woman dressed in a banana costume dancing and singing on Park Avenue in New York began chanting "Freud is an arrogant fraud" when she discovered I was in psychoanalytic training at the time.

It feels as though the general consensus within and outside of the psychoanalytic community is that we are an arrogant bunch. While it can be reassuring to brush these comments off as envious and aggressive projections, there is of course a long tradition of arrogance in psychoanalysis that is a painful reality. The "origin story" of psychoanalytic societies began with arrogance—Freud's ruthless methods of alienating colleagues who had contrasting perspectives, most notably his notorious "secret committee" which demanded absolute professional and personal submission with secret rituals and loyalty rings, are the most striking example (Groskurth, 1991).

The tradition of arrogance continued in America with the ascent of psychoanalysis as the dominant model of understanding human psychology, beginning in the 1930s and reaching its zenith in the 1950s through the 1960s. In 1957, in the highly influential and widely published *An Elementary Textbook of Psychoanalysis*, Charles Brenner confidently wrote: "At present, interest in psychoanalysis is expanding … it seems likely that the current interest in psychoanalysis on the part of psychiatrists and associated workers in the field of mental health will continue to grow" (p. 243). This obviously did not come to pass.

The barring of nonmedical specialties from psychoanalytic institutes and training (which Freud was against) and the infiltration of psychoanalysts to prestigious posts in medical education cemented psychoanalysis as an elitist occupation. This culminated in an overt use of psychoanalytic theorizing to validate heteronormative cultural values including homophobia and sexism (Dean & Lane, 2001; J. Mitchell, 1974). It also led to psychological reductionism and ignoring complex genetic and organic factors most notably in autistic and psychotic disorders (Shorter, 1997). The ascent of psychoanalysis in America also led to widespread arrogance within training institutes, promoting submission to orthodoxy and a squelching of curiosity and creativity (Kernberg & Michels, 2016). Other notorious examples of arrogance include numerous boundary violations of patients (Gabbard & Lester, 1995), greedy pandering to the rich and elite (Shorter, 1997), and racism (Powell, 2012).

The unfortunate outcome of this widespread institutional arrogance is an enduring stain on the image of the psychoanalyst, who is usually depicted in the stereotype of a snobbish, fussy, and privileged white male who makes his living barely engaging with his equally wealthy clients who could care less. This is in striking contrast to the psychoanalysis that is radical in its understanding of human relationships and the unconscious as well as traditions within psychoanalysis that promoted social activism and freedom of thought and expression (Danto, 2005; Gaztambide, 2019). As Aron and Starr (2013) state bluntly in their book *A Psychotherapy for the People: Toward a Progressive Psychoanalysis*:

In the 1950s, at the height of its success in America, psychoanalysis made a choice. The choice was to define itself narrowly in order to maximize its status and prestige. A sharp divide was erected between analysis and psychotherapy, thinking it would keep the treatment pure ... and that it would justify high fees and the high cost of training. It seemed like a good thing to make psychoanalysis an elite medical subspecialty. It became a high cost, high class, elitist, exclusive practice for an exclusive clientele. (p. 28)

It must be said, however, that everything written above has been documented and discussed at length by scholars within and outside of the psychoanalytic tradition. But to focus on this obvious overt arrogance in our profession feels too convenient and smug—the joy of sneering at others for their arrogance at a distance is seductively pleasurable. What about our own arrogance and how it affects our practice on a daily basis? I have a colleague who every year after our annual psychoanalytic meeting turns to me and remarks, "What a bunch of arrogant narcissists!" I always laugh and unwittingly encourage his comments but secretly feel anxiety about my own cringeworthy moments of arrogance with my patients and wonder how much we gleefully project our own arrogant fantasies into "these narcissists."

The realization of my own arrogance continues to be a painful experience, which is not easy to tolerate. Mostly it was pointed out to me by my patients who, within their rights to speak freely, did so in a manner that exposed me to my blind spots of arrogance that were disconcerting and always unknown to me in the moment. As psychoanalysts, we cannot ignore our context or our history of internalized elitism and arrogance within ourselves. By doing so, we risk losing our ability to access vulnerability in our patients and become overly identified with mastery and success. In its identification with the wealthy and elite, psychoanalysis dissociated its vulnerability by projecting it into other "lesser forms" of psychotherapy and onto "difficult" patients, leaving psychoanalysts in the role of identifying with the heroic and masterful (Aron & Starr, 2013).

In this chapter, I would like to focus on our arrogance in the clinical setting and its effects on our clinical work with patients. I believe we all have vulnerabilities that lead to arrogance that emerge in our work with patients. This is a way of avoiding the temptation of declaring some individuals arrogant (usually referred to as "the narcissists") and others—conveniently including oneself—as free of arrogance. We can then allow a more nuanced and personal vantage point in which to explore the ways in which arrogance plays a role in the clinical encounter.

For heuristic purposes, one could separate out transient arrogance that emerges in the analytic space at various times, and a more fixated chronic arrogance that can be pervasive which informs the approach to one's work, often in a manner unknown to the analyst. Faced with the terror of the unknown, the analyst can retreat into a state of arrogance, enclosing herself in an internal cocoon with what is known, excluding and being condescending to the patient (Zimmer, 2013). The analyst is then "reduced" to arrogant ways of being to ward off the bewildering and frightening state of affairs that is erupting in the room.

## Defining arrogance

Arrogance results from a narrow-mindedness in feeling and perception (Akhtar, 2009). Two aspects of arrogance that are present are a combination of superiority and a feeling of certainty, which leads one to feel a heightened sense of narcissistic satisfaction and omnipotence. There is an exciting, seductive, at times sexual experience of knowing and being self satisfied—"It makes perfect sense, after all." There is a curious lack of anxiety or conscious shame and there is a feeling of clarity of being comfortable in being the knower. One's tone of speech transforms into a more declarative and omniscient quality.

Self-righteousness is often present. Others observing this arrogant behavior often perceive smugness, stubbornness, and rigidity. Arrogance is a nonreflective self-state of mind. It is only after it is pointed out or reflected upon later that one realizes one has in fact been arrogant. Unfortunately, it is perceived first by the person who is the recipient of the arrogance, who often is rendered to feeling inferior and demeaned. This leads to him feeling oppressed and forced to either agree with the arrogant person or rebel against him. In the "arrogant moment" the arrogant person is not aware of this, specifically the aggressive and demeaning aspects of his behavior, which reflects a kind of stupidity. "I'm not being arrogant, I'm just stating the truth—why are you getting angry?" Another quality of stupidity in the experience of arrogance is how complexity and depth of human experience are reduced to linear "facts" and rigid concepts, which will be discussed further below.

Bion's celebrated and enigmatic paper "On Arrogance" (1958) describes a constellation of widely dispersed, seemingly unrelated references to the triad of arrogance, stupidity, and curiosity in a seemingly neurotic patient who has psychotic mechanisms of thought. Differentiating life-affirming self-respect from arrogance, Bion states that the analyst should be alert to references in the patient's associations to arrogance, stupidity, curiosity, or suicidality, with either the patient or the analyst inhabiting these attributes unconsciously.

Bion attributes this to a "psychic disaster" involving the patient's relation with an early caregiver who is was not capable of the infant's need for emotional containment and communication via projective identification. This results in a disruption of the patient's ability to create a creative and meaningful link in relationships through genuine emotional communication.

Most importantly, this "disaster" is also being recreated *between the analyst and patient* by the way in which the analyst is communicating to the patient—it is the analyst that is arrogant. By insisting on verbal communication and advancing conceptual ideas and theories, the analyst does not have access to the patient's most primitive and vital forms of communication via projective identification; she cannot "stand it," this unbearable affective way the patient is expressing himself to the analyst via the countertransference (Bion, 1958; Carveth, 2017).

In the analytic situation, this causes a retreat on the part of the analyst and patient—for the analyst, the retreat is often to her relationship with analytic theory and her current way of thinking about the patient. This is truly a "disaster" because it disrupts the analyst's ability to have access to and be with the patient's most primitive and vital forms of communication (Zimmer, 2013). The analyst's ability to live with and contain the patient's unbearable psychic suffering via projective identification in the countertransference is vital to create a safe "home for the mind" for the patient to contain and transform his unspeakable pain (Cooper, 2016; Reis, 2020; Spezzano, 2007). Arrogance in the analytic field blocks this vital process of unconscious communication.

Below I will describe the various ways in which the analyst's arrogance can have this effect, including the analyst's disruption in an ability to experience failure and the depressive position; a collapse of depth, surprise, and a sense of awe that arises when arrogance takes hold; a disruption in curiosity; and the hidden pleasures of arrogance in seduction.

## Arrogance, failure, and the depressive position

Uncertainty and the possibility of failure haunt the practice of psychoanalysis. The well-worn analytic clichés of our profession being "impossible" speak to how difficult it is to constantly be in a position of not knowing and grasping the unconscious, which of course is never fully knowable. The terrifying uncertainty and intimacy of the clinical encounter can easily lead to arrogance as a way of warding off the possibility of failure and not knowing.

The analyst's capacity to contain doubt and the unknown was notably described by Bion (1970), using the term *negative capability*. This term, borrowed from the romantic poet John Keats, is "when a man is capable of being in uncertainties, mysteries, doubts, without any irritable reaching after fact and reason" (Keats, 1817, quoted in Sedlak, 2019). This ability to tolerate the pain and confusion of the unknown, rather than imposing certainties upon an ambiguous or emotionally unbearable situation, is lost in arrogant states of mind. In contrast to being with our "doubts, uncertainties, and mysteries" about our shortcomings and failures, we find ways of trying to make sense of them by preserving our sense of certainty at the patient's expense.

We are especially vulnerable to this collapse into certainty when we experience failure or stumble in our work. Our patients invest an incalculable amount of time, effort, and money in us and it must be admitted that feeling the effects of our failures is truly an unbearable experience. It must be someone else's fault! As A. Goldberg (2012) notes about his failure to help a patient:

> Somebody else was to blame for this sad state of affairs, and that somebody was probably the patient. Or anyone but me. I later learned that almost everyone who fails as a therapist has a storehouse of excuses that can be called up, examined for usefulness,

freely discarded, and just as freely embraced. Failure has no friends. (p. 29)

The temptation to resort to some form of arrogance in these situations is incredibly high. Importantly, it is not just the failure of our individual cases that we feel the need to protect ourselves from, but often in the ebb and flow of a daily session where our patients are letting us know how we are failing them in direct and indirect ways all the time.

Probably the most common way of warding off these unbearable communications from the patient is to lapse into blaming the patient in subtle (and sometimes not so subtle) ways. Casement's (2002) wonderfully honest book *Learning from Our Mistakes* highlights this:

> Psychoanalytic practitioners sometimes slip into a position of arrogance, that of thinking they know best. Thus, when something goes wrong in an analysis, it is often the patient who is held accountable for this, the analyst assuming it to be an expression of the patient's pathology rather than perhaps (or at least partly) due to some fault of the analyst's. It is unfortunate that analysts can always defend themselves by claiming special knowledge of the ways of the unconscious. But analysts can become blind to their own mistakes. And even more importantly they can fail to recognize that it is sometimes the style of their clinical work itself that may have become a problem for the patient. (p. xv)

Because of our training and our supposed "understanding of the unconscious," we can easily fall into the arrogant trap of using our explanations as a cover for our anger and confusion in not knowing. In fact, our training in making connections often can be used in the service of expressing our arrogance:

> Let's face it: analysts and therapists become experts in making connections. We can connect almost anything with anything! And we can always use theory in support of this, however wild these connections might be. Then, when things don't fit exactly, we can assume the patient is employing whatever forms of defensive thinking best lend themselves to our own way of seeing

> things … in fact, we can use theory in almost any way we wish. And yet there are times we are bound to be wrong. But if our style of working is to be too sure, it can become a real problem for the patient when the analyst is getting it wrong. (Casement, 2002, p. 4)

This can lead to various forms of arrogance that we are all familiar with, including lecturing the patient, offering unempathic reassurances, interpreting the patient's actions we do not like as resistance or aggression, or offering practical suggestions and strategies that are of limited use. Experientially, we often feel this in ourselves in moments when we are being clever and overeager to provide explanations.

Britton and Steiner (1994) refer to this phenomenon as an *overvalued idea* on the part of the analyst, an error that is made based on biased or partial understanding due to the defensive needs of the analyst, which is usually accompanied by "a sense of excitement and achievement" in the analyst (p. 1070). While they stress the importance of interpreting "with conviction," they insist on the "capacity to entertain doubt" and a willingness to commit the analyst "to a point of view which seems right at the time, and yet be willing to relinquish this view if subsequent evidence demands it" (p. 1070). They acknowledge the need of the analyst's facing up to the experience of "doubt, guilt and other feelings associated with the depressive position" as an inevitable part of the analytic process.

This yearning we have for a sense of coherence and cohesion in our understanding is a form of what Lacan (1957) refers to as *méconnaissance* or misrecognition. This can be the exciting "I know exactly how you are feeling" experience when it all makes sense to us (Hook, 2018). These "I get it" moments are precisely moments of *misrecognition* based on an illusory gestalt that is more about our fantasies of perceiving wholeness and perfection to avoid incompleteness and lack. In this way, understanding and knowledge are inevitably linked with a false sense of certainty.

The impulse towards false certainty with our understanding of patients often occurs in moments when we experience what Jurist (2018) calls *aporetic emotions*, emotions that are experienced as vague and lacking specificity. We know we feel something, but are uncertain as to what that feeling is, and the effort to understand what we are feeling lacks meaning or coherence. Jurist reminds us that we often experience emotions only partially, and often as a confusing mixture of several emotions simultaneously to varying degrees of clarity. To ease this confusing and unsettling experience, we can resort to simplistic explanations for what is happening in the clinical encounter based on our wish to find some emotional coherence.

These concepts emphasize a well-known dictum in analytic work: Interpretations and our interventions with patients should not be used as an opportunity for us to demonstrate our cleverness. Menninger notes clinicians "need to be reminded that they are not oracles, not wizards, not linguists, not detectives, not great wise men who, like Joseph and David, 'interpret' dreams—but quiet observers, listeners and occasional commentators" (Menninger, 1958, p. 129; quoted in Kahr, 2020). I would add that being a "quiet observer and occasional commentator" can also be a way of safely maintaining a distant and implicitly omniscient stance.

Brett Kahr (2020) describes a few infamous and surprising historical examples of falling short of this ideal of negative capability in esteemed psychoanalysts we admire. In the 1930s, a young American in analysis with Helene Deutsch recalled that on one occasion, Deutsch made an interpretation, upon which the patient reflected carefully and then replied, "Maybe." The young American then reported that Helene Deutsch replied in a way that was a "most opinionated and cocksure answer … not maybe but yes" (Kahr, 2020; quoted from Menaker, 1989, p. 148).

Donald Winnicott's wife Clare Winnicott, in analysis with Melanie Klein, on one occasion described a dream to Klein, who then gave her an interpretation of "its secret meaning fully twenty-five minutes in length" (Kahr, 2020, p. 184). Another analysand of Melanie Klein's, Dr. Clifford Scott, reported that Klein had such a long interpretation of a dream she had to write it down—and took two sessions to read it out to him! (Kahr, 2020, p. 185). Clearly, keeping in mind how the analysand was taking in what was happening was not considered here.

Casement offers a useful and pragmatic method of combating this tendency by cultivating our ability to perform "trial identifications" with our patients, considering from the patient's point of view either what we have said or what we are thinking of saying. The analyst's comfort in working also means that he thinks about the unintended effects that his participation is having on the patient (Casement, 2002). This combats the tendency towards facile cleverness and unempathic interpretations based more on our inability to tolerate our patient's unconscious communications.

However, overly identifying with the patient can lead to arrogance as well. If the analyst feels too identified with or guilty towards the patient's lived experience, others can become the target of blame and arrogance. I am always struck in clinical case discussions and also in my own countertransference with patients how tempting it is to blame the patient's pathology on their parents or significant others and transform these living human beings into caricatures of bad objects. In one case conference I attended, the discussant, a psychoanalyst, spoke about how a patient described her parents leaving the bedroom door unlocked when she was a child and how she had felt she had hidden access to their lovemaking because of this. A member in the audience gasped loudly and shouted, "What the hell were they thinking! They are not truly parents!" Where did this outrage come from?

This is not to underestimate the trauma and unspeakable pain that is disclosed to us by our patients about their past. I am speaking more to the manner in which we can arrogantly transform people into almost cartoon-like caricatures for our own arrogant purposes, which is to maintain a feeling of moral superiority, leading us to forms of "stupidity."

The truth of the matter is that our work as psychoanalysts is by default incomplete, unsettling, and uncertain. Living in this "depressive position" and reflecting on ways in which we move towards omnipotence to avoid incompleteness and loss is essential to help our patients attain this as well. Even after a productive and meaningful analysis, our lives will continue to "be out of joint" in a certain way. The analyst holds this unsettling narrative in the service of helping the patient to better contain this as well (Cooper, 2016).

This capacity to accept incompleteness allows us to be more available to our patients' interiority and their struggles with living in "ordinary misery." Arrogance can block our patients' ability to access this within us. This also applies to our internalized representations of our teachers and theories—arrogant clinging to a particular model or theory without an understanding of its incompleteness maintains an omnipotent and walled off analytic stance.

This ability to acknowledge the depressive position and live in incompleteness and to tolerate failure and uncertainty should not be confused with self-deprecation or self-loathing. When we choose not to blame the patient or the people in the patient's life, the "bad" one often turns out to be us. The temptation to give in to self-loathing and vicious self-attacks seems to be a professional hazard for almost all of us at some point. As we see in our patients, attacks on oneself often involve an unconscious grandiosity that is arrogant as well. As Cooper notes, self-criticism "rests between the silent acceptance of disappointment or shame on the one hand and on the other a clearly disproportionate level of grandiosity about our ability" (2011, p. 21).

## Arrogant compliance and the collapse of depth and surprise

A deepening analysis is a jarring and confusing experience for both the analyst and patient. What we were first told as "facts" about a person initially become infused with conflicting meanings and emotional truths. Michael Parsons (2000), reflecting on this process, writes:

> … to genuinely enter into a patient's viewpoint can involve an unexpectedly profound shift of position. We know something matters. Then something happens which jolts us into seeing it afresh and throws into relief just how much it really does matter. We did realize it was important and we knew why, but from where we stand now, seeing how acute its significance truly is, our previous attitude cannot help seeming a bit bland and superficial. (p. 36)

This experience gives rise to the possibility of surprise and depth. Psychic depth can be viewed as the experience of what is known in the foreground (subject) surrounded by a less articulated and perceived background which is "there" but its meaning is unrealized at the moment, an affective resonance and fullness that would otherwise be flattened (D. B. Stern, 2015). Depth allows for emergent possibilities and the possibility of surprise, a crucial element in the psychoanalytic process. A cocreated analytic space of depth and emerging possibilities allows for experiences of awe, surrender, and vulnerability, crucial in the analytic process for the patient to be able to reclaim a sense of self and psychic experience (Ghent, 1990).

Because of its emphasis in domination and solipsism of knowledge, arrogance collapses depth into a flattened experiential world. In contrast to the patient feeling instinctively safe to surrender and have faith in their relational freedom with the analyst, he feels he must submit to whatever worldview the analyst feels is correct. Boredom, cocreated stupidity, and dry intellectualized interpretations can follow from this. The arrogant analyst has "figured it out" and has already understood what has unfolded—she just has to convince the patient what she is saying is correct.

Aron (1996) usefully differentiates the terms mutuality and symmetry in the analytic encounter to describe these dilemmas. *Mutuality* implies reciprocation and unity through interchange, and is in a dialectical relationship with separateness, difference, and autonomy. *Symmetry*, in contrast to mutuality, implies a degree of equality or equivalence between two people. Aron argues that while psychoanalysis aims to be a mutual process (he gives examples of mutual empathy, mutual affective involvement, and mutual enactments) the relationship must inevitably be *asymmetrical*, because "It is the patient seeking help from the analyst and it is the patient coming to the analyst's office and paying the analyst; it is the analyst who is the professional and is invested as such with a certain kind of authority and responsibility" (1996, p. xi). When an analyst is arrogant, this inherent asymmetry is leveraged for the sake of power, and mutuality is falsely assumed based on an insistence on the analyst's assumed "knowledge."

Holding both the authentic mutual and asymmetrical aspects of the work implies the analyst must abandon the idea that she has superior knowledge over the patient's psyche and bear the tension and difficulty in these competing positions. Meaning is arrived at through a "meeting of minds," with each interpretation or understanding subject to continual and multiple reiterations between both the patient and analyst (Aron, 1996).

Bromberg (2012) notes the differences in the impact this has on the patient's mind:

> Each patient analyst couple must strike its own balance of safety and risk, but for any patient, confrontation with the analyst as a separate center of subjectivity will be most enlivening and safe

if the analyst is not trying to figure things out on his own and then using his own truth about his patient as a means to a good therapeutic outcome. The more an analyst's communication is based on sharing his subjective experience because he wants it to be known, as opposed to wanting it have a preconceived impact on his patient's mind, the more it will be felt by the patient to be "affectively honest." (p. 103)

As stated above, when an analyst takes on the position of the knower "figuring out things on his own," the other is reduced to either submitting or rebelling. For a vulnerable patient desperate for help, this is an impossible choice. Casement (2002) notes, "Patients get put in a situation where they do not have sufficient say concerning what is being assumed about them, and they may be at times exposed to interpretations that cannot effectively be challenged. They then have little choice but to leave that analyst or capitulate."

An attitude of arrogance where the analyst's reality is correct can go unrecognized by the analyst but have profound effects on the patient. Interpretations made outside the alive quality of the cocreated experience between patient and analyst often feel like indoctrination and produce compliance. In order to survive and protect their inner world from being invaded and colonized, the patient develops a false compliant self that can go unrecognized. This leads to a deadening of the lived experience between the analyst and patient and a lack of depth in the material. "What is happening between us, what I think it is, nothing more, nothing less." Depth, ambiguity, and mystery collapse—the analytic space becomes flat. "There is a certainty about things that are perhaps left uncertain, because uncertainty allows possibility. The possibility of new meanings is shut down. Things are what they are, nothing more" (Stern, 2015).

This type of false compliance in a two-dimensional space destroys the opportunity for playfulness. Giving out interpretations as unquestionable "facts" to the patient does not give them the opportunity for them to join in and play, "kicking it around whilst offering other angles that could also be considered" (Casement, 2002). In order for an interpretation not to be indoctrination, the patient has to creatively make use of it, changing and transforming it in the process if needed.

## Case example

Molly, a fifty-seven-year-old magazine editor and a mother of two boys, ages eighteen and sixteen, began treatment with me after her analyst of fifteen years passed away. Despite a fifteen-year treatment, Molly was significantly impaired in her ability to function due to severe anxiety and somatic symptoms including intermittent pains in her throat and neck with no clear medical cause. She spoke in a rapid and loud fashion, staring straight ahead with only intermittent eye contact, with a flurry of complex ideas and verbiage that often caused me to feel confused and worried that I could not understand her. I began to also feel ashamed that I could not keep up with her complex ideas and thoughts that seemed to relentlessly take up the entire session.

Most of her associations involved angry struggles with her ex-husband and her two sons, both of whom had developmental delays and behavioral issues. Molly felt overwhelmed by her sons' needs without any help, which reflected her past as well. Molly was the fourth in a family of eight, born prematurely with a neurological disorder that affected her ability to walk. Growing up, Molly watched her brothers and sisters play together without her. Her mother was diagnosed with lupus and was often bedridden. When she was awake, her mother preferred the company of her eldest son, leaving Molly alone with her books.

I felt flooded in our sessions together without the ability to self-reflect and contain much of what she was saying. I found myself resorting to often repeating what she was saying back to her in an effort to enter her experience or make empathic comments, neither of which seemed to resonate with her. I also tried to help her make connections between her past experiences struggling with her own disability and maternal neglect and her current overwhelmed helplessness in helping her sons with their needs and how possibly she was searching for help here with me in a similar way. None of my comments seemed to reach Molly. She would usually not pause after I spoke and make a few intellectualized remarks about possible connections between her past and the present and then continue to talk about the details of her daily struggles with her two sons and her ex-husband's unavailability. She also explicitly ignored any comments about our relationship and its emotional meaning for her.

This went on for several months and I began to feel trapped in a flatness of being with her—it seemed there were no moments of emergence, surprise, or depth in our relating with one another; she was "just reporting" the events as she saw them. I found myself starting to become more and more "stupid" in my comments and not able to think or reflect clearly. As my thinking became more superficial, my tone changed as well, although I only realized this in retrospect. The tenor and quality of my voice took on a more authoritative and oracular quality, which was simultaneously definitive and superficial.

In one session, Molly began by talking about how a friend was supposed to take care of her two sons for her to have a night out. Right before leaving, her friend called and canceled. Molly was enraged and spent the session ranting about how she had no one in her life that can help her with anything, and that she felt others around her were either incompetent at helping or did not care. Unable to contain myself for some reason, I blurted out, "Which one am I to you? Incompetent or uncaring?" Molly looked visibly shaken by this comment. She paused for a moment and then replied, "It's always about you, isn't it? You and your goddamn ideas about me."

I was taken aback by this comment—she had never been so honest, and had not expressed anger towards me prior to this. Uncertain how to respond, I mumbled, "Thank you for the honesty ... I'm open to hearing more about what you feel." I noticed my tone of voice change to a more submissive register as I said this and realized how we were locked in a distant relationship with one another, with me occupying the role of an arrogant and domineering other which now was reversed. It dawned on me that I was unconsciously attempting to imitate, and possibly be a caricature of her previous analyst (he was more senior to me) with my authoritative tone of voice.

Over time, Molly began to open up more about her feeling that I was not connected to her inner world and that I was arrogant in my tone of speech and method: "I feel like you are just saying things out of a book sometimes and want me to agree with you. I don't feel you're a real person here, but you're all I have right now." I began to realize I saw her somatic pain as "an idea," not the actual bodily suffering she was enduring. Later in the analysis she also expressed her grief and anger over the sudden death of her analyst who she loved deeply and how seeing me brought up intense longings for him, and how it was painful to allow herself the vulnerability of receiving help.

This vignette brings up the importance of the "tonal elements" in our speech in the ways we communicate with our patients. This is infrequently discussed in the literature, which is surprising considering how vital it is. The vocal quality and prosody of our voice, our facial expressions, and our posture and body language often convey much more to the patient than the content of what we say (Kahr, 2020). Kahr wisely notes that our interpretations (I would add all of our interventions) should ideally be verbalized in a "musical manner, so that the tone of voice and speed of delivery" are suitable for the patient. Of course, when we inevitably fall short of this ideal, it is crucial that we are curious and mindful of what is happening.

## Curiosity and arrogance

Another consequence of my arrogance with Molly was a disruption in my curiosity and genuine interest in her. My curiosity was "stupid" because it had to do with trying to "figure it out" with Molly in an arrogant fashion. What I did not appreciate was my inability to bear what Molly was experiencing and trying to communicate to me nonverbally, her lived "catastrophe" of the devastation of her loss and somatic pain.

In his discussion of arrogance, Bion (1958) describes a constellation of arrogance, stupidity, and curiosity as a "psychic disaster" that is linked to psychotic parts of the personality. At first glance, this is puzzling because curiosity—the drive towards obtaining knowledge and understanding—is essential to the psychoanalytic process for both the analyst and patient. Curiosity promotes and allows for the patient to internalize self-reflection, mentalization, and wonderment for their inner affective life. Why would Bion add this to a "disastrous" constellation including stupidity and arrogance?

Curiosity considered carefully is a complex and multidetermined process that can have varying configurations and motivations. Authentic curiosity speaks to our desire to face and seek the truth, and the wish to understand ourselves and others (Jurist, 2018). This desire, like all desires, can have other motivations as well that are often unknown to us. For heuristic purposes, one can separate two distinct types of curiosity that can be forms of an arrogant curiosity: pseudo-curiosity and instinctual curiosity. Pseudo-curiosity is rooted in the sense of a person not genuinely interested in understanding others—he is more interested in his own ideas being of value. Akhtar (2009) notes, "A peculiarly naive curiosity about others accompanies this dehumanization … however this curiosity does not express a genuine wish to understand others. Rather it reflects puzzlement about their motivations on the part of an individual who has little knowledge of his own intrapsychic life" (p. 26). The pseudo-curious analyst wants to understand what they already believe to be true and needs validation of their own internal truth—curiosity is a method proving their own ideas as correct. Listening is perversely transformed to finding out his or her own thoughts inside another person's subjectivity. The other experiences this as oppressive and dehumanizing and the subjective alterity of the other is abolished. As one of my patients said to me, "You may think you are asking me a question, but what you are really doing is trying to prove to yourself that you have the right answer to the question you just asked."

Instinctual curiosity has to do with our libidinal investments inherent in curiosity—how we, in effect, "get off" on being curious. In his discussion of the triad of arrogance, stupidity, and curiosity, Bion reinterprets the Oedipus myth as a quest to "lay bare the truth at any cost" rather than a focus on incestuous and patricidal wishes. This aggrandized search for the truth regardless of the consequences lays bare the instinctual aspects of curiosity that can predominate in an arrogant state of mind which is oblivious to the consequences of this overzealous curiosity (Zimmer, 2013).

This type of instinctual curiosity can take the form of the analyst relentlessly searching without regard to a patient's boundaries or a private space in mind away from the analyst's intrusion. As Poland writes in his wise and measured essay "The Analyst's Approach and the Patient's Psychic Growth" (2013):

> There is an inevitable tension built in between those two forces: curiosity to satisfy oneself and respectful regard for the needs of the other … what is specifically psychoanalytic in clinical work arises from the force of the analyst's curiosity tamed in the desire to utilize that curiosity primarily in the service of the patient …

the tension between the analyst's curiosity and wish to advance inquiry, on the one hand, and the analyst's staying sensitive to the patient, on the other hand, demands creativity on the analyst's part. This is a large part of what makes clinical work an art … it was from the marriage of curiosity with respect for the other that clinical psychoanalysis was born. (p. 834)

This taming of instinctual curiosity in the service of the patient with respect is lost in an arrogant state of mind that disregards the need for privacy from the analyst's penetrative searching.

## Case example

I met Lewis, a twenty-four-year-old chemical engineer, for an initial psychotherapy and medication consultation. He reported a history of panic symptoms and long-standing inhibitions surrounding social relationships. He identified as bisexual and had several close friends but had difficulty initiating or sustaining relationships with romantic partners. Being an only child, Lewis felt he was very close to both his mother and father but felt his mother could be at times anxious and controlling. As a varsity gymnast in high school and later in college, Lewis felt a great deal of pride in his physical athleticism but also struggled with his body image as "slender and petite" for a man and often felt shame around viewing his body in pictures or being in locker rooms where others could see him not fully clothed. In our initial consultation, Lewis brought in a novel with him that piqued my interest, *The Brief Wondrous Life of Oscar Wao*, by Junot Diaz. I had recently read the book and found myself wondering if the book had meaning for him in regards to his intimate relationships with others. I felt a strange pressing need to ask him about it for unclear reasons at the time. Towards the end of the session, I finally said, "I noticed what you are reading—does it bring up any feelings or thoughts?" He looked slightly uncomfortable and said, "Why, is it important?" I replied that if the book brought up any feelings or thoughts it could be a way of us understanding her inner world better. He half-heartedly seemed to agree with this and afterwards I felt the session went well. Later that night, Lewis called, asking to speak with me. He wanted a referral for another therapist. "I think a woman therapist would be a better match for me—I don't feel comfortable speaking with a guy about these things."

It seemed my unchecked curious inquiry frightened him. Without being consciously aware of it at the moment, my interest in Lewis was laden with instinctual wishes to know about private areas of his life without the restraint of respecting his privacy. My wishes to know about his private life also may have enacted a seducing other that was overstimulating and frightening to him.

## The seductive power of arrogance

In contrast to the deadness that arrogance often imposes on others, there are clinical moments when arrogance can induce thrilling and seductive fantasies enacted by the analyst and patient. Arrogance can be an intoxicating and exciting experience—full of omnipotence and certainty, the analyst conveys a special kind of magical power that can evoke powerful fantasies. These can include sadomasochistic fantasies of erotic submission and rescue fantasies of being saved by a powerful other. The analyst's certainty and conviction combined with an often unconscious wish to assume a sexually exciting authority position can provoke these scenarios.

The enactment between arrogant male analysts and female patients has been extensively written about elsewhere (McWilliams, 2011). Subtle forms of these types of seductive arrogance occur, however, on a more frequent basis in a variety of clinical situations that is often overlooked. Enjoying the potency and thrill of being in a position of power is not just something that narcissistic men experience—we are all prone to these seductions.

## Case example

Jenny, a forty-nine-year-old physical therapist of Haitian descent with a history of alcoholism and depression, began treatment after her youngest child graduated high school. After her son's graduation, she began drinking heavily at night to cope with the emptiness of the house and her emotionally unavailable husband who was absorbed in his successful roofing business and hobbies. Jenny felt comfortable in the treatment right away and began to make improvements over the first several sessions. She had never been in psychotherapy before and felt "liberated" being able to speak freely to me.

Growing up, she felt her mother was superficial and fragile and often felt the need to play the role of a caretaker for her. Jenny felt more of a connection with her domineering and powerful father who was often absent because of his own struggles with alcohol. I found myself feeling affectionate towards her and pleased with myself that she took to the process of therapy so quickly. After several months of psychotherapy, her drinking had significantly reduced and she was able to begin to make changes in her life that she felt proud of. A few weeks after Jenny began working again, she left a desperate message on my voicemail asking me to call her back. I happened to be free when she called and was able to call her back right away. She disclosed that she had a relapse of drinking alcohol and was frightened about falling into old patterns again "before I saw you."

The conversation was brief but had a lasting impact on her. At our next session, Jenny felt "incredible" and the fact that I was so responsive to her needs made her feel better than she had for years—"It was as if a veil was lifted off of me." As she was saying this to me, even though intellectually I knew that this moment had to do with her experience of me that was informed by her transference and early longings as a child, it felt incredibly validating and exciting to have had the power to have helped her this way. I found myself secretly congratulating myself on how my relationship with her had such an impact on her.

After this session, her depression improved but she began to drink heavily at night again, leading to hangovers during the day. What I was not able to see at the time which later became clear was that her relapse occurred after she began working as a physical therapist again and she was deeply conflicted about her autonomy and power. Her fantasies of me being an omnipotent rescuer were enacted in ways I was not fully conscious of until later in the treatment, when I began to realize the manner and way in which I spoke to her conveyed a firm but loving father who wanted to take care of her and protect her—this way of relating to me helped her feel more safe and secure and also protected her from her wishes to be assertive and powerful which frightened her. Later in the treatment, frightening and guilt-ridden sexual transgressive feelings also emerged that were implicit in this paternal protective fantasy.

Kahr (2020) rightly questions the often implicit assumption that if we make a "brilliant" interpretation or intervention the analyst has actually succeeded in her task. With Jenny, it seemed my interpretations were more an enactment of an unconscious masculine and phallic activity which created a sense of excitement in both of us. My arrogance was a way of "taking charge" over the treatment and her mind, as opposed to us working closely to ensure that interpretations were coconstructed (Kahr, 2020).

Ellen Pinsky (2017) devotes an entire chapter entitled "The Potion" on this dynamic in her emotionally courageous and erudite book *Death and Fallibility in the Psychoanalytic Encounter.* She compares an analyst who succumbs to "the charms of his own person" to Bottom, the "loquacious clown" in Shakespeare's play *A Midsummer Night's Dream,* who becomes an "ass headed man" after drinking a potion which makes him charismatic and attractive to the enchanted fairy queen Titania (p. 39). Pinsky warns that a charismatic and grandiose analyst, basking in the erotic transference, "drunk on the love juice, may feel justified by 'the charms of his own person' and their effect—he believes he is himself a bit magical, charismatic" (p. 39) This form of grandiosity, despite being potentially exciting for both the patient and analyst, "prevents or supplants mourning," and "punishes trust."

With this being said, we should be careful to not be "arrogant about arrogance" and dismiss it as something that needs to be completely avoided. In the ebb and flow of our clinical work, we are all vulnerable to an onslaught of frightening affects, fantasies, and defensive reactions to them. It can be frightening, uncertain, and confusing. We all succumb to psychic retreats (Steiner, 2011a) to protect ourselves from this emotional storm of intimacy and I would include a position of arrogance as a method of coping in this way.

## Healthy arrogance?

Arrogance also has a developmental aspect as well. This is described in the literature on the narcissism of adolescence and its defensive and adaptive purposes for the development of self-esteem and conviction (Blos, 1965). Perhaps there is a similar developmental arc for psychoanalysts in training—allowing oneself to experience and be a person of authority with conviction is an important aspect of our work that requires time to be comfortable with.

In conclusion, to put it simply, we should have a place to be honest about our arrogance. When left unchecked and unspoken, our arrogance can persist unconsciously in the form of chronic self-doubt or secret envious attacks on others. When we are uncomfortable with our own desire for power and clinical conviction, we can easily descend into anxiety-ridden defensive arrogant stances with patients and colleagues without being aware of it. Being conscious of our arrogance, in the end, allows us to hold it lightly and frees us from being flat, stupid, and self–important—at least for a moment.

CHAPTER 2

# Racism

*What we want is to walk in the company of man, night and day,
for all times. It is not a question of stringing the caravan out where
groups are spaced so far apart that they cannot see the one in front,
and men who no longer recognize each other, meet less and less and
talk to each other less and less.*
—Frantz Fanon, *The Wretched of the Earth*, 1961, pp. 237–238

Due to the seismic events over the past several years, including the horrific murder of George Floyd and the glaring visibility of racial hatred and disparity worldwide, everyone seems to be engaged in some form of discussion about race and racism. These discourses are many, and include the dynamics of power and privilege, the urgent need for tolerance and empathy, "white fragility," and naming and describing various forms of implicit bias.

Difficult conversations about race have the possibility of opening up areas that before were closed down and invisible to us. Because racial trauma, discrimination, and prejudice rely on complicity in silence, engaging in open discussions about these topics disrupts our tendency to avoid and minimize the entrenched forms of racial trauma and injustice that surround us (Powell, 2021).

A consequence of this, however, is that thoughts about "race" and "racism" are often rendered as intellectualized abstractions to be discussed and theorized about outside of the consulting room, "enjoyed" as an interesting topic of conversation. What happens in the racist encounter—to our living bodies, our souls, and inner life when the political meets the visceral (Mbembe, 2016) in the heat of the experience—is left out. My hope is that this chapter will allow a space for the struggle and conflict inherent in the experience of racism and prejudice in the *clinical encounter*. In this spirit, I will start with a personal moment outside of the office and how it became a "live wire" in the consulting room.

## A racist moment outside the office

I was driving my son and daughter home after their summer camp in New Jersey on a hot summer day in the afternoon in August. My mind was wandering and I was distracted by the day's events. I gradually noticed a large black Jeep in my rear-view window with two young white men with baseball caps behind me swerving their car back and forth and quickly flashing their lights. Living in New Jersey, I am used to this kind of rudeness—aggressive driving is a part of daily life. I felt annoyed but resigned to just letting them pass. Suddenly, the jeep accelerated to the side of my car and then slowed down, demanding my attention. I turned my head to look towards them and the passenger through an open window gave me a menacing look and raised middle finger. "Go the fuck back to your country, asshole!" he yelled as the Jeep sped away. I got a look at the back of the Jeep as it drove off: old New Jersey plates, a sticker of the American flag, and a huge "Make America Great Again" sticker on the back window proudly displayed.

At first, I was stunned. I couldn't think clearly, my head felt cloudy, and I could feel a throbbing sinking sensation in my stomach. I felt helpless and shamed and my face felt hot and my body was trembling. I reflexively looked back at my children and they seemed completely oblivious to what had happened, both of them just sitting there. I then felt an incredible impotent rage within me swell up. Hateful words flooded my mind, including "white trash." I wanted to chase that car, smash into it, find out where those men lived and hurt them and their families. A wave of paranoid anxiety then hit me—"What if they come back? What if they try to hurt my family?" I pictured the car and their faces contorted in hatred and my stomach dropped again. The rage was unbearable. For a moment, I thought I could maybe find out who they are. I could post a video on YouTube of what happened, humiliate them and their families, get an army of people to find them and ruin their lives. A part of me shamefully wanted to exaggerate what happened to create a greater effect on the person listening to the story. People would say it wasn't a big deal. It only lasted for a second, not even a minute. I am safe and my children are safe. Maybe it did not even happen the way I thought it did. It could have been much worse. Despite these thoughts, the shock of that moment and an uneasiness in the pit of my stomach stayed with me.

## A racist moment arrives at the office

A few weeks later, I was in the midst of a psychotherapy session with Kay, an intelligent and poised Caucasian thirty-four-year-old married woman with a degree in finance and a mother of two young children. Kay worked part time at home for a well-known financial firm and at the time of this session was struggling with the transition to suburban life—she missed being in Boston, the city where she got her master's and had her first job. She felt overwhelmed by the responsibilities of her life: raising two children, balancing a career, and struggling to connect emotionally and sexually with her husband John, a successful invest-ment banker who was raised by a prominent Republican family in the community where I work.

Kay was in twice-weekly psychoanalytic psychotherapy with me for about eighteen months and presented initially with lifelong symptoms of depression which included a pervasive self-doubt, a lack of being able to experience pleasure, and a persistent sense of unease that she was not doing something right. She worried others in her social circles had a bet-ter life than her—a more fulfilling marriage, more polite and emotion-ally regulated children, and a nicer and stylish home.

Kay began the session describing an argument she had with her hus-band John the day prior to the session. She described a dynamic we had often talked about before—she felt overwhelmed and resentful of the fact that John often came home late and did not seem appreciative of the sheer amount she had to do with her own job and the two children while he was away. Kay often expressed her frustration towards him by making passive aggressive comments and mocking his inability to take care of the children without her help:

Kay: I think we are both just exhausted. I know I pick fights with him that are unfair, we've gone over this before. He's got this long commute on that disgusting Northeast corridor line. It's gross, and he hates it. It makes all these stops and these people get on the train and crowd in making it so tight and smelly. You know, those … (*Kay suddenly looks visibly uncomfortable and grimaces.*)

Me: You made a face there.

Kay: I don't want to say it, okay. How did I end up talking about this? *Those Indians* … I was going to say, but you're Indian! I shouldn't have said anything. Now I feel stupid. I hate this. You tell me to say whatever is on my mind, and not to censor myself, and now I'm saying this and you're going to say I'm a racist. Dammit!

A racist fantasy crashes the analytic field. Obviously, we have entered dangerous territory and it has taken us both by surprise. Racism, a traumatic historical and political act of violence, infiltrates the intimate space of the consulting room. This is by no means a surprise—the personal and political feel so dangerous, yet closely linked in our lives today it would be surprising if this did not occur between us at some point in our relationship.

## Unbearable truths about racism

I want to focus on my reaction to her comment and her subsequent associations and how it affected my ability to think and stay in an open and curious state of mind. Psychoanalysis has always emphasized verbal freedom—to speak the unspeakable, to cultivate the courage to put into words what before felt forbidden and shameful. Our commitment to survive and contain our patient's most unbearable affects and fantasies is an essential aspect of this process. While this is of course true for experiences of racism as well, I would argue there is a combustible and dangerous quality to these moments for both the analyst and patient that intersect areas of culture, privilege, and trauma that put particular challenges on the analyst's ability to stay with the patient.

As psychoanalytic therapists we have to confront two facts about racism that feel impossible to resolve—the profound destructive effects of racism and its disturbing ubiquity. To take up the first fact, it is obvious that racist states of mind have caused individual and societal harm on an unimaginable scale and the experience of a racist attack is traumatizing.

Although cultural, historical, and sociological accounts of race often neglect the subjective impact of racism on the individual victim that psychoanalysis can ideally address, psychoanalytic theorizing can also minimize the profound impact of race and racial relations in individuals and communities who have been oppressed and humiliated by a culture shaped and created by colonization and slavery. (For a detailed discussion on the complex and surprising history of psychoanalysis and topics of race and racism, see Danto, 2005; Gaztambide, 2019; Plotkin, 2018; Powell, 2012.) Reducing racial dynamics to familial and developmental psychoanalytic concepts may defensively aim to evade this uncomfortable reality, as opposed to illuminating the ways in which destructive racist societal structures are internalized by the experience of racialized subjects.

The psychiatrist, activist, and psychoanalytic theorist Frantz Fanon powerfully describes a moment like this on a subway when he was suddenly identified as "a Negro." Fanon (1952) feels like he is being "sealed" into a "crushing objecthood," as if encased by his own skin. He apprehends others' gaze as a sensation running over the surface of his body, "first burning and shivering with cold, that cold that goes through your bones." A lifetime of moments of racialized attacks like this creates dissociative splits in our experience, fragmenting the fabric of our intersubjective spaces of meaning and connection with others.

In these racist moments inside and outside the office, I felt a similar painful gut level response that is difficult to fully articulate. Psychoanalyst Narendra Keval (2016) writes, "To be at the receiving end of this type of animosity is to experience something that cuts deep and gnaws away subtly at your sense of self, sometimes signaled by a visceral response that something is not quite right, a feeling in the guts that one has been, or is being, misused" (p. xviii). In the same passage he writes: "There is a rupture in one's continuity of being—that sense we all have control of our insides, of what uniquely sets 'me' apart from 'them,' the ability to not let the other to march in and take possession of the self along power lines" (p. xvii). This experience of rupture and violation "in the guts" leaves the therapist vulnerable to specific countertransferences and enactments that will be described in more detail below.

This trauma of racism collides with another unbearable truth—we all have racist beliefs and fantasies lurking in the recesses of our minds, often unknown to us. All of us have the potential to be racist. Racism is not created out of external societal structures, nor is it purely intrapsychic, but rather both shape and call upon each other.

Conscious and unconscious racist fantasies often organize our relations to one another through encounters with difference and the mysterious "other," and in moments of vulnerability, psychic distress, or threat racist structures are deployed towards this "other." Fonagy and Higgitt (2007) note that prejudice regulates affect—it can be an antidote to overwhelming and massive mental pain and shame. There is something disturbingly "normal" about our unconscious method of creating a stereotyped other to project hateful fantasies onto when we are under duress. In his illuminating and groundbreaking work on psychoanalytic approaches to racism, Fakhry Davids (2011) writes: "How many of us who are otherwise tolerant and/or liberal on racial, ethnic or cultural matters cannot, when we look hard enough, find an intolerant bigot or racist lurking in some corner of our minds?" (p. 42). Similar to there being unconscious psychotic areas of functioning within us, prejudiced and racist aspects of our personality exist in all of us as well (Akhtar, 2007).

The universality of racism and prejudice is one rare area of convergence in multiple fields of research including psychoanalytic theory and case formulations, critical theory, social psychology, cognitive neuroscience, and cultural anthropology. Research and clinical experience clearly demonstrate that we all carry implicit racial biases and racist prejudices, including unconscious racial biases against our own ethnicities and ourselves (Banaji & Greenwald, 2013).

However, from a psychoanalytic perspective, theories of "implicit racial bias" are incomplete due to their emphasis on rationality and cognitive processes and minimization of affects, drives, and unconscious fantasy. Racism is not solely a problem of cognition: If this was the case, racism could be ameliorated by additional knowledge or understanding (George & Hook, 2021; McGowan, 2021). As McGowan (2021) states bluntly, if racism was merely a cognitive bias, then "armed with this understanding, to correct our unconscious bias, we just need a little diversity training that teaches us that our biases are unfounded" (p. 32). This is clearly not the case—there is something inherently tenacious and unyielding about racist states of mind. What are missing from these discourses are our unconscious affective and libidinal *investments* in racist fantasies, which will be discussed more below.

In our current cultural climate, it is dangerous and forbidden territory to discuss our racist fantasies. Being called a racist is one of the most frightening and shameful labels to carry: "the Scarlet R." It is associated with being evil, immoral, dirty, and dangerous—in a word, a sin. There is a strong temptation to project our racist fantasies onto others to relieve this tension, enjoying the pleasures of moral superiority. The temptation to project our own racism self-righteously onto our patients or an "other" outside the consulting room and stay "pure" is immense. This is especially dangerous because of its impact on growth and genuine exploration in psychoanalytic therapy. We might never meet a full blooded "racist" in our clinical practice, but if you do not come across any racist or prejudiced parts of your patients or yourself, you have not been paying close enough attention. The challenge for us as clinicians is to acknowledge and explore racial biases, ignorance, and privilege that take place within the therapeutic dyad (Powell, 2018).

I hope to demonstrate some of these dilemmas by describing my session with Kay after her racist associations and the potential struggles and opportunities that occurred between us.

## Getting "called out"

Let us return to the moment before she connected her associations with my ethnicity. Kay was discussing being exhausted and picking fights with her husband John when he gets home and she seems to identify with John's "dirty commute" and her associations to dirtiness, "tight and smelly" crowds, very visceral associations to "those people." She then blurts out the connection: Indians are dirty, and that "I am Indian." There is a painful jolt of being exposed in my brown skin—I suddenly feel exposed and attacked. The concept of interpellation can help describe a moment like this—the process by which subjectivity is "hailed into being" by another who has authority (Dimen, 2011). There is a strange dissociated "me/not me" experience: It's me she's saying is "Indian," but it doesn't feel like the me I live in. The common expression for this gets it right on a visceral level: I got "called out." An essential part of me, my ethnicity and skin color being a massive form of self-disclosure out of my control, feels exposed. What before was unreflected on and precon-scious comes into sharp focus without me asking for it.

The racist episode described above and the cumulative weight of my identity being a focus of negative associations and attacks contributed to the pain of this jolt into consciousness. At that moment it was dif-ficult for me to think clearly and I felt a hot flush come over me similar to my experience with the men in the Jeep. I think this may have been why I commented on her facial expression, "You made a face there." I felt called out and self-conscious, and perhaps I unconsciously wanted to "call her out" and reduce the level of shame and discomfort I felt. A similar process may be occurring in "call out culture"—victims of rac-ist attacks calling out their attackers online and in the public sphere— "You people have called me out and shamed me for my ethnicity and skin color and now I'm going to show you how it feels to be called out and shamed."

## The face and words don't match

Let's continue with the clinical material.

Kay: You tell me to say whatever is on my mind, and not to censor myself, and now I'm saying this and you're going to say I'm a racist. Dammit!

Me: I can tell what you just said made you uncomfortable.

Kay: Of course it did [*sighs, visibly upset*]. Now I'm the racist, the Trump supporting racist in your office. And I know you hate me for that. How can I say these things to you without you hating me? I can tell by the look on your face you are annoyed.

Me: You don't feel I can tolerate your feelings and thoughts about this? Like you said, this is the place to say whatever is on your mind.

What my face was communicating was obviously in conflict with what my words were trying to convey! bell hooks notes that people of color "quash a killing rage" as daily insults like this pile up (hooks, 1995). Reflecting on this moment, what I said was based on needing to ease this painful rage that came through in my facial expression, although I was not fully conscious of this at the time. This "racist moment" moved me into a concrete and dualistic state of mind that is very familiar to anyone who has been in a situation like this: "Should I speak up and defend myself—my ancestors, culture, family—or let it go?" One is trapped in either direction. If you speak up, you will be accused of blowing things out of proportion, being hypersensitive, and getting angry over something that's not a "big deal"—now it becomes "your anger problem" and the "attacker" feels victimized and assaulted by you. This often descends into blaming, guilt, and shame on both sides (Davids, 2011). If you "let it go" and ease the discomfort between you and the other you are left shameful and impotent with an uneasy sick feeling you did not stand up for the most vital aspects of your existence: your family, your skin, your homeland and culture—the sounds, tastes, and smells of what you hold most precious to you and that you feel pride in.

In a therapeutic moment, the stakes can feel even higher. As Kay said, this is her space to speak the unspeakable, to put into words what in most places is forbidden and off limits. This freedom of psychic movement, to explore, to be curious and open hearted to all aspects of who we are feels blocked in these states of mind between the therapist and patient. It felt like a kill or be killed moment for both of us, with no intersubjective or moral third holding the space for reflection or curiosity (Benjamin, 2018).

## Racist or racial fantasies?

Racism is based in our collective cultural fantasies, specifically fantasies about the skin and the body. Crucial to racist states of mind is an essentializing belief that skin tone or bodily features signify a fundamental "otherness" and a lower status of being. This "epidermalizing gaze" which endows the skin and the body with meaning creates the fantasy of "the truths of racial difference from the other's body" (Stephens, 2014, p. 322).

Several authors on this subject, notably Keval, make a distinction here between racial and racist fantasies. Racial fantasies, according to Keval, are fantasies that notice the ethnic characteristics of others and are motivated by a curiosity that can signal a wish to explore the self in relation to others. In my office, the transferences to my ethnicity and skin color have spanned an incredible range—I can be a dangerous terrorist, a sexless nerd, a mysterious powerful guru, or a house servant all in one day! Racial fantasies in these moments sometimes feel more exploratory—the intersubjective space is alive and open to possibility, despite the projections and displacements in the associations (Keval, 2016).

In contrast, racist fantasies aim to thwart and damage, closing down opportunities for intimacy. These fantasies are better described as racial enactments (Leary, 2000) or "racist states of mind." There is a wish for absolute certainty, and an atmosphere of brutality, omnipotence, arrogance, cruelty, and shallowness (Keval, 2016). The primary defense here is massive projection. The therapist becomes the hook on which to hang the psychic material that the patient finds too difficult to think about—with Kay, it was Indians as dirty, smelly, and "gross." Racist states of mind and racial enactments exist within an interpersonal relational space that feels shut down and concrete, with no sense of curiosity, playfulness, or freedom for both the therapist and the patient. The therapist struggles to resist pressures to feel either defeated or to give in to sadistic impulses of wishing to triumph over the patient. Striving to think or understand under this kind of fire is very difficult and it seems there are countertransference obstacles in every direction. This is analogous to Bion's distinction between "degrees of normal" and "pathological" projective identification, the latter being motivated more by attacks on linking and destructiveness (Bion, 1959). What is crucial is the struggle of the patient's and the analyst's ability to contain and be with what is unbearable for both of them.

Returning to the clinical material, my face betrayed the violence and hurt I felt towards her, but my words were attempting to reassure her and to disown and dissociate the violence within me. The angry dissociated part of me in the moment would have said: "*You* are the dirty one! Your people and your white skin have caused so much pain, you should be the one who feels ashamed, not me!" Although I was not fully aware of it at the moment, I wanted Kay to feel like the weak, powerless, dirty nothing that both she and those men in the Jeep made me feel. Davids notes: "One is cast as a virtuous victim of racism, survivor and savior, by virtue of having experienced it one becomes the authority on racism." This is a way of allowing the victim to have revenge, to "do" something. The atmosphere turns hostile and suspicious. He continues: "It is impossible to think, and political correctness becomes the order of the day. We feel divided into friends and enemies" (2011, p. 49).

Paradoxically, this only barely conscious struggle led me to become overly solicitous and welcoming of Kay's racist thoughts, in part to mollify the violence within me towards Kay and to ward off any more attacks from her. The term "psychic airbrushing" (Crastnopol, 2015) and excessive niceness applies here: a way of communicating only half-truths and engaging in a cover up of denial that is "positively retouched, made to look better than normal," in effect saying, "I welcome your racist thoughts! They don't bother me." This led to a disruption of authentic emotional communication between us for a moment. The gap widened between who I truly am and how I want to be known. Reflecting on this moment now, it may have been more useful to encourage her to stay with her associations and our mutual discomfort, noting the truth in her noticing the emotional reality in my facial expression. Alternatively, I could have made more analyst-centered responses (Steiner, 1993), listening and commenting on her experience of me and my reaction to her.

## Escape into the transference?

Returning to the clinical material:

Kay: Say what's on my mind? God, how can I really? You therapy types are liberals. And I'm a shitty racist.
Me: First it was the Indian guys on the train that were dirty, and then it seemed to be me, now you're the "shitty one?" All of this dirt and shittiness sounds like the words you've used about your father.

To provide some context here, this was not the first time Kay had associated to my "dirtiness." In past sessions, she had commented on my unfashionable clothing, and my messy and dusty office.

Some background about Kay is also important: Kay described a chaotic home growing up in rural Georgia despite outward appearances of wealth and stature. Her parents both worked full time and she was raised by nannies, one of whom was brown skinned, whom she was very attached to at the age of five. This nanny left suddenly at Kay's age of ten with no prior warning, leaving Kay with no way to mourn her loss. She described her mother growing up as either absent or often in emotional distress sobbing in front of her and in constant agony over her father, who despite his financial successes had a lifelong opiate addiction and multiple affairs which culminated in him being diagnosed with HIV when Kay was in high school. In our sessions, she would often refer to her father as a "gross and disgusting human being—I want nothing to do with him." Her husband John's family upbringing, with its traditional Protestant values of family, church, and nationality, appealed to her greatly—it felt "pure and clean," but she often felt a nostalgic mixture of longing and hatred toward the dysfunction of her old family and the South which felt familiar and more viscerally alive to her. She recently had been opening up about a closeness to her father until puberty when she began to notice him looking at her breasts in a sexual way and discovered evidence of his illicit affairs and drug abuse by going through his dresser drawers when he was away.

Clearly, there are multiple meanings here of what "dirty Indian" means to Kay. The inspiring and courageous psychoanalytic works of Dorothy Holmes (1999) and Aisha Abbasi (2014) in particular discuss the transferential and the genetic origins of racism in their clinical encounters with patients. Both discuss how racist fantasies can be defensive sadistic attempts to evade unbearable experiences of helplessness, shame, rage, and narcissistic injury originating from early childhood experiences (Abbasi, 2014; Holmes, 1999).

Much of this certainly applies to Kay's associations. Being dirty has connections to her father's dangerous sexuality and the trauma it caused her and her family. She experienced her erotic life as "dirty," partially because of her identification to her father and her fears about her body responding sexually, which has transference implications to my skin color. Her "clean and white" husband responding to her sexually also brought out these painful and frightening connections.

There is also her attachment and sudden loss of her brown-skinned nanny which evoked her fear and shame over needing to rely on others for emotional support, which she defended against by becoming demeaning and critical of people she depended on. This was the dynamic happening with her husband John that she was speaking to prior to her association of the "dirty Indians"—depending on people is "dirty."

Being a "dirty Indian" also had deep meanings for her own identifications with being a "dirty foreigner" as a Southerner in a wealthy New Jersey suburb. She wanted to be more "white" and less dirty as a form of ethnic and familial purification. Here being "white" is a cultural fantasy of total purity and privilege (Hamer, 2012). She called her hometown in Georgia a "shithole" and felt the people there were "ass backwards trash." Joining her husband's "more white and sanitized" privileged family carried the fantasy of escaping his dirtiness but carried with it a disavowal of her cultural heritage, pride, and family.

Returning to my session with Kay, this "overvalued idea" about the connection between her father and dirtiness came to me unbidden at that moment and I chose to say it (Britton & Steiner, 1994). Although the comment was probably in the right ballpark, it missed the mark because it had a defensive quality to it. I think I used the comment reflexively to move away from the pain and rage of the moment between us to something more familiar and intellectualized—the connection between the transference and her father. I could feel my anxiety lessening as I made the comment—we were in familiar psychoanalytic territory now. Staying in the painful and uncomfortable moment between us could have led me to being more open to the multiple possibilities to be curious about in her associations to "the dirty Indian."

## Envy of white privilege

Another reaction I had to Kay at this moment was a hateful but barely formulated envy of her white skin and the privileges it afforded her. I could feel this only in retrospect and at the time it was sensed as an aching sense in my gut, a sick visceral "less than" feeling. The therapist's envy towards the patient has rarely been discussed and is more prevalent than our clinical literature would suggest (see Chapter 6 on Shame). In this moment, my feelings of her having more wealth, status, and privilege than me brought forth my own internalized racism against my brown skin and heritage, which may have also led me to defensively move away from the discomfort between us to a more intellectualized interpretation.

It may have also reflected her own enviousness of how she experienced me through projective identification—later in treatment, she was able to put into words her hatred and anger towards her compulsive need to "sanitize" herself and felt envious that I seemed to be very comfortable in my "dirty and dusty office."

## Envy, idealization, and unconscious racialized debasement of Blackness

Stepping aside from the clinical material with Kay, it would be worthwhile to describe other forms of envy that can emerge in working with patients of different racial and ethnic backgrounds. Racially envious countertransferences can sometimes manifest as an idealization of a community of color that masks unconscious racist fantasies. Analysts are by no means exempt from such fantasies and these were made manifest with another patient of mine, Sandra (who I discuss in more detail in Shah (in press)).

I felt an "uncomfortable envy" towards Sandra, a twenty-one-year-old undergraduate student of Korean and African American descent. Within the competing and conflicting intersections of power and privilege between us, in one phase of our work together this envy manifested itself towards Sandra's African American heritage. Her father's wealthy African American family was historically rooted in United States history, with a legacy of activism and intellectual rigor that was in contrast to my own family of origin. Although I "pass" as an American and grew up in the United States from the age of two, on a visceral level my experience is of being a first-generation immigrant without deep roots to my country.

It took some time and considerable discomfort to see in my work with Sandra how my "uncomfortable envy" of her African American heritage masked more forbidden and unbearable feelings about Sandra's

Blackness. Eager to "get it," consciously I felt solidarity with both of us being people of color while envying her status in a prominent African American family. What was more disturbing, covered over by my claims of recognition and communion, however, was my uncomfortable visceral repudiation of her being Black, based on my own internalized racism of Blackness and my denial of the intergenerational trauma of slavery and negation of African Americans as human subjects in American and world history (Wilderson, 2020).

My envy of her family and culture was a fetishized and defensively idealized fantasy of Blackness based on my own racial insecurities. Growing up in an interracial community that was predominantly divided between African Americans and individuals who identified as white, I struggled to understand my place and how I fitted in as being brown skinned but set apart from the dichotomized racial struggles in my town. Although I idealized and admired African American culture, feeling close to people of color, underneath this enthusiasm in part was a devaluation and an implicit denigration of Blackness. I superficially conflated being a person of color with being Black, which denied the structural basis of racism based in the trauma of slavery and the abjection of the Black body, ignored Asian racist attitudes towards skin color, and relegated Black people to a "zone of non-being" (Fanon, 1952).

This difficult phase of our work together involved Sandra's anger at me for not getting her experience as separate from my own, envy towards me for being "totally Indian" and not subject to the racial debasement African Americans endure, her envy of her cousins she perceived as "more Black" than her, and a fantasy of wishing she was "purely Black" to feel accepted and close to her father and his family. Sandra and I struggled to both feel and know her African American ancestry in an embodied way, as well as mourn the fantasy of this essence of Black "racial purity" as an attempt to heal the wounds of her biracial experience and the wish for wholeness that is inherent in all racial fantasies (George, 2016).

## Excluded from the motherland

To return to Kay, in addition to envious racialized enactments, racialized countertransference experiences involving melancholic exclusion and jealousy can also involve fantasies of competition with a pure "mother-land." This occurred after my interpretation about Kay's associations of dirtiness relating to her father.

Kay: Say what's on my mind? God, how can I really? You therapy types are liberals. And I'm a shitty racist.

Me: First it was the Indian guys on the train that were dirty, and then it seemed to be me, now you're the "shitty one?" All of this dirt and shittiness sounds like the words you've used about your father.

Kay: Yeah, that's true. He was gross. Sighs. I don't know. I feel lost in all of this. I just wish I didn't say any of it. (*Kay becomes silent for about a minute.*)

Me: That was a long pause.

Before I interrupted Kay's silence, I felt a deep sense of exclusion in the silence between us. I was alone and cast out. My mind wandered to the Jeep rushing past my car: "Go back to your own country," he said. "Dirty Indian" flashed in my mind. So it's their country, not mine. They belong here. Where does that leave me? In our silence together a sense of melancholia fell over me that I needed to interrupt with words.

Although America is a country I love, the only country I feel is truly mine, what persists is a sense of dislocation—I am almost American like Kay, but not quite. Eng and Han use the terms "mimicry" and "racial melancholia" and to describe this experience—the Asian American is a model minority mimicking the successes of white privilege without the political and cultural legitimacy of being white. A racial melancholia hangs over this partial success and partial failure, a ghost-like lingering of being similar but never the same (Eng & Han, 2019). I felt jealous of Kay's ability to be with America in a way I can never be.

Being alone and cast out has resonances with Kay's experience and her racist associations to me as well. Racism can be a defensive reaction to primitive experiences of exclusion, jealousy, and shame. Keval (2016) discusses the concept of the "racist scene." He describes this as a particular strategy of revenge in a racist state of mind. The racist feels jealous of the minority's relationship to "his mother-land." It's his country, his mother. The thought of this intruder enjoying the pleasures of being with his motherland creates unbearable hatred and jealousy—he creates a fictionalized pure and unspoiled past before the dirty immigrants ruined this blissful union between him and his pure mother. Now he is the oedipal loser, helplessly watching his motherland and immigrants in union with one another, stuck in the primal scene. He must reverse this humiliating loss—he will make the immigrant the excluded other. They are the "dirty outsiders" and his union with his mother-land is pure and virtuous (Keval, 2016).

Hook (2021) adds a crucial element to these types of racist fantasies by describing the racist as one who fantasizes that the minority has stolen his "libidinal treasures." "Libidinal treasures" are ideas or objects imbued with narcissistic value, encapsulating what is most vital to us. In the racist fantasy, "the other" has stolen this from us; they are enjoying what we feel is deservedly ours. What pains the racist most is how the other is *enjoying* themselves. Racist fantasies are then passionate ways of expressing the ways in which "the other" has stolen our enjoyment (George, 2016; Žižek, 1992). The racist then collapses into "passionate hating" that unconsciously links them with the despised other. The brown-skinned Indian, "enjoying" the pleasure of his body and odor, crowding and taking over the space of the train, excluded Kay and left no room for her own erotic and sensual desires rooted in her body, her "dirty" Southern background and her brown-skinned nanny.

Although material about this from Kay came later in our work together, my feelings of exclusion in the silence with Kay and my reverie to the Jeep and the words "Go back to your country" may have also reflected her own experiences of exclusion and isolation with her father and his lovers. These mysterious women were "the dirty ones" who drew her father away from her and the family. Other triadic conflicts included the birth of her older brother when she was three, her mother's constant preoccupation with her father's infidelity and drug use at her expense, and her feeling excluded from the "in crowd" in boarding school who were interested in sexuality and drug use.

## Can playfulness exist in a moment like this?

Kay: I was just thinking about how strange this is. I feel out there, exposed. I don't know what you're going to say or how you are going to react to what I said. Are you going to fire me?

Me: You could see on my face I was a bit rattled by it, but it seems we are on this dirty NJ train together! Let's stay with what you're feeling and see where it goes.

Kay: So you *were* rattled! I knew it. Okay, okay, I think I get what you mean. It's just awkward as hell to do this.

I wanted to conclude by talking about a potentially difficult topic not often discussed in the analytic literature—the use of playfulness clinically in racist states of mind. We are all familiar with the immense literature on the necessity and importance of playfulness and play, inside and outside psychotherapy, and actually with all mammals (Panksepp, 1998). Play creates a psychic space between our inner world and external reality, taking place paradoxically neither strictly in only our imagination or reality. It allows for movement between opposites, paradoxes, and variations of meaning and truthfulness (Winnicott, 1992). When you are being playful you can try on an experience or fantasy as opposed to being oppressed by it or taken over. Being subjected to a racist state of mind and also the experience of feeling you are a racist collapses this transitional space into a mode of psychic equivalence—"You are what I fear." In this mode, one either has to comply or resist (Benjamin, 2018).

Patricia Gherovici's (2021) thoughtful and sensitive work with a Dominican patient named Mercedes demonstrates this delicate balance between playfulness and tact. Gherovici described Mercedes's hostile racist fantasies towards the "Jewish ladies" that she shared a yoga class with, whom she felt were ruining her sacred space. Recognizing the way in which Mercedes's racist associations were about her fantasies of longing for unspoiled perfection, Gherovici *managed to make her laugh.*

> The distance created by the laughter was sufficient to uncover the fragile construction supporting her racism. An eruption of laughter during a session had lifted the racist paranoia, pointing to the fact that her hatred would hide and reveal at the same time the minor differences that are exacerbated … to create a sense of identity. It also reminded her that when you laugh you can see your own rigidities and introduce subjective flexibility. (p. 198)

Returning to my clinical moment with Kay: Was my comment to her about being on the "dirty New Jersey train together" merely a defensive and masochistic way of warding off the aggression in the field between us? I think that seeing it this way would be limiting. My comment opened up a space between us to not *just* feel in the grip of our anxiety and anger. This is a difficult topic, however, because there are dangers of being too playful. Using the image of two animals playing, we can make a distinction in play between "a nip" and "a bite" (Bateson, 1955; Benjamin, 2018). When excitement and aggression increase, the heightened affective arousal can destabilize the paradoxical holding of something as both from the traumatic past and not the past. Power relations reveal themselves. The bite feels real, and playfulness becomes teasing or outright viciousness. But the opposite is true as well. Our fear over aggression can limit our ability to authentically engage—"We may be so fearful of biting that we can't properly engage the other's nip" (Benjamin, 2018). In this moment between Kay and me, my comment did help us get unstuck and allowed for her to be more playful with her projections of dirtiness. We were in it together, hurt but still on the train.

# CHAPTER 3

# Dread

> *The therapist must be capable of feeling real desperation on behalf of another as well as on his own behalf; it is when we are bereft of every artifice and prop, of all the technical support our profession gives, that we are close as possible to reality.*
>
> —Farber, 1958, quoted in Bolognini, 2004, p. 99

"Hi, I don't think I want to do this anymore. I can't stand feeling this way. If I do decide to end things, please know it was not your fault. I just can't live like this anymore. No need to call me back if you don't want to."

I received Brenda's voicemail walking out of my office Friday afternoon. As I was listening to this message, a feeling that can only be described as dread gripped my insides, rendering me unable to think. Brenda, a fifty-eight-year-old musician with two adult children, was reaching out to me in desperation and immense psychic pain. Two years ago, her husband, a well-respected artist, had committed suicide after intimate details of his infidelity were publicly revealed online. Inconsolable following her husband's death, Brenda descended into what she described as a "private hell" of alcohol, drugs, sexual acting out, and self-mutilation.

After several brief inpatient hospitalizations (prompted by suicidal thoughts and intoxication), multiple medication trials, dialectical behavioral therapy (DBT), and electroconvulsive therapy (ECT), Brenda continued to struggle with intense mood lability, chronic suicidal ideation, and an inability to function and take care of herself. Her twenty-four-year old son, in psychoanalytic treatment with a colleague of mine, reached out for help and Brenda began psychoanalytic psychotherapy and psychopharmacological treatment with me three times weekly. Brenda often had intense urges to cut her body and also described a variety of ways of committing suicide including using her friend's shotgun, jumping off the roof of her apartment complex, and hanging herself. She felt this most strongly after being abandoned by one of her numerous lovers or when her children canceled their plans with her. Despite this immense suffering, she was committed to our work together and did not miss any appointments—alongside her suicidality, she also felt a will to live and not leave her children parentless.

I felt a great deal of respect and admiration for her, but her propensity to act on her wishes to die often left me frightened. Moments of dread with Brenda were there from the start—before receiving this voicemail, I had experienced some form of it countless times in the one year we had been working together. I never felt dread so palpably, however, as the day I listened to this voicemail. The feeling pervaded my body and my mind, taking me over and rendering me immobile.

This chapter is about our dread—as clinicians, therapists, and healers being faced with what feels unbearable to us and to our patients. We do not often discuss these experiences directly, perhaps out of shame, but also because these dreaded moments bring up what we as clinicians would like to forget. I will argue that allowing ourselves to feel and explore our experiences of dread by facing up to them honestly opens up possibilities for being with and approaching what otherwise would be unbearable for ourselves and our patients. An episode of dread with our patients signals a present and future apprehension of facing an unbearable emotional truth we have not adequately mentalized and accepted. I favor a "no holds barred" search for our raw emotional reactions that take the form of dread. What we cannot tolerate seeing and feeling within ourselves, we cannot find in our patients (Coen, 2002, 2013; Eshel, 2019; Searles, 1986).

Although experiencing dread is always a possibility in the intimacy of the analytic space, I want to focus on several unbearable realities we have to contend with as clinicians that ordinary life often obscures. Being with suicidality, murderousness, profound helplessness, punishing and disavowed guilt, and disturbing erotic desires that do not comply with our self-image are, remarkably, part of our ordinary day and can be experienced as dread.

Reflexively, we will want to flee these dangers, either by dissociating or by emotionally removing ourselves in some way. Staying with our dread, naming it, and getting to know what is happening within us, although challenging and not without its own dangers, allows us to potentially better tolerate what we are feeling and what our patient is implicitly communicating to us. What was earlier dreaded can then be experienced as an anxious apprehension that can be reflected on and even momentarily felt as awe. Following Bion, Sedlak (2019) notes that a central aim of psychoanalysis is to help our patients transform suffering *from* a mental state to being able to suffer *with* what they are feeling without resorting to evading these painful emotional truths. Confronting our countertransference dread means facing up to difficult aspects of external and internal reality with our patients and ourselves and being able to bear them emotionally, which is the essential work of emotional transformation and growth. Gradually, with time and effort, our struggle to be present with our patients' most devastating experiences without defensively closing down or avoiding them allow them to be more contained, lived through, and felt within the interconnected experience of self-with-other (Eshel, 2019).

## Experiencing dread

To explore the experience of countertransference dread, it would be worthwhile for me to slow down and describe my reaction in detail the moment I listened to Brenda's voicemail. Hearing the words "in tears … I don't think I want to do this anymore … I can't stand feeling this way," I immediately felt a visceral bodily reaction. Unbidden and out of my control, I physically reacted violently to the words. I could feel my heart rate quicken and a state of nausea gripped me. Symptoms of this primal fear response share some overlap with what is often described as a panic attack. In contrast to an episode of panic anxiety, however, the experiential quality of dread has an ominous and foreboding quality with a distinct sense of something terrible and loathsome happening. Also, in contrast to panic attacks, which often involve experiences of attachment, loss and separation (Busch et al., 2012; Panksepp, 1998), experiences of dread are usually experienced as something threatening and horrendous getting too close. Examined closely, it often feels as if one is being attacked with an apprehension of another attack, accompanied by a visceral fear of some mutilation to the self or the body. This intensity and affective overloading that one experiences in a moment of dread differentiates dread from more "ordinary" forms of countertransference anxiety.

In his illuminating work on dreaded self-representations, Koch (2000) sums up the experience of dread:

> What these diverse experiences [of dread] have in common are their suddenness and unexpectedness; the potential arousal of intense and overwhelming affect; the loss of one's agency, experienced as acute helplessness or being out of control; and the threat to one's sense of what is "real," either in oneself or in the external world … each of these traumatic situations is the stuff of nightmares. To glimpse these events and feelings in some form of remembering bears the danger of repeating and reexperiencing them. Such a danger becomes defensively anticipated, i.e., dreaded, lest one is once again overwhelmed by the unmanageable. (p. 300)

## Psychoanalytic theory and dread

There is no straightforward or definitive definition of dread in Freud's writings, and there are shades of various meanings expressed by the German words he uses to describe comparable experiences, including "fear" (*Furcht*) and "anxiety" (*Angst*) which run into difficulties with translation and conceptual blurriness. Adding to the complexity and messiness in defining these terms, they have everyday meanings as well as established psychiatric and medical diagnostic definitions (Laplanche & Pontalis, 1973; Strachey, 1962). We usually use the word "anxiety" to describe a particular state of expecting danger or preparing for it, often not being aware of what that danger is. Fear requires a definite object of which to be afraid (Laplanche & Pontalis, 1973). Dread could be conceptualized as an intense hybrid of fear and anxiety—fear because of it often being caused by a specific event or trigger, and anxiety because of its nameless foreboding and menacing quality.

Dread is an experience in the paranoid-schizoid position (Klein, 1948), with the qualities of persecutory anxiety, splitting (the object of dread is experienced as "all bad" and we are helpless innocent victims to this assault), and an inability to symbolize and reflect on what we are experiencing—causing us to feel flooded and under threat. These qualities of dread usually have unconscious underpinnings of early trauma, projected aggression, and persecutory guilt, which I describe in more detail below.

The experience of being unexpectedly overwhelmed and surprised by dread is partially captured by Freud's use of the term "*Schreck*," often translated as "fright" (Strachey, 1962). Lear (2005) notes that the term "dread" better captures this experience of "*Schreck*." In contrast to fear and anxiety, which are states of fearful preparedness for danger, dread is what happens when one is unexpectedly overwhelmed: "The normal defenses against danger do not have time to operate, and one is overwhelmed by dread" (p. 156). I would add that dread includes a foreboding and menacing sense of the future, accompanied by an extreme reluctance to face the emotional truth of the situation. When we say, "I dread ..." we are implicitly communicating that we do not want to face up to what feels too unbearable to approach. Dread thus exists both in the present moment and in the anticipated future.

Dread of course has roots in the past as well, and the majority of psychoanalytic theorizing on dread describes its origins in childhood trauma. Sullivan (1953) described what he called "the uncanny emotions," namely, dread, awe, loathing, and horror, which, if conscious, would threaten the very core of one's being. Formless and wordless, these emotions hold disowned and projected experiences he named "not me" aspects of the self—originating in childhood fears and traumas. In his classic paper "Fear of Breakdown," Winnicott (1974) theorized that a patient's fear of mental breakdown is a fear of returning to an actual breakdown in the form of "primitive agonies" from early life which he relates to failures in the "facilitating environment" against which the infant is defenseless, being dependent upon that very environment to provide support in the form of the mother. He noted "anxiety is not [a] strong enough word here" (p. 103) for these agonies. Khan (1972, 1974) discussed the infantile roots of dread in the danger of surrender and dependency and the vulnerability of being one's true self. Bion's (1962a) evocative term "nameless dread" speaks to the infant's experience of a mother's not accepting her projections of primitive emotional states related to fears of dying. In the mother's refusing to accept this unbearable experience, the infant "reintrojects, not a fear of dying made tolerable, but a nameless dread." This term has been used in contemporary analytic theorizing to describe the experience of the analyst's being temporarily unable to accept and contain the analysand's dread and primitive mental states through analytic reverie. The analyst's experience of this "nameless dread" is an intersubjective experience with the patient, which hopefully will help the analyst metabolize these primitive mental states and transform them into a more manageable, digestible experience for the patient (L. Brown, 2019). This intersubjective perspective on dread is the starting point in my discussion.

## Escaping from dread

Let us return to the moment I picked up Brenda's voicemail. Without warning, I was flooded with dread as I thought about returning Brenda's call. She had concluded her message with "No need to call me back if you don't want to," which was how she usually ended her messages—clearly a "loaded" and potentially deadly ending to the voicemail. Unable to think clearly, I momentarily had an urge to take Brenda up on her offer not to call her and flee from the relationship. I wanted the whole situation to "just go away," and felt helpless and trapped with Brenda and her endless misery. These reactions, while shameful and difficult to feel consciously (and to write about), are crucial to being with and healing patients with chronic suicidality.

Countertransference errors are often made when we are not honest about our wishes to abandon our patients and the unconscious guilt that accompanies this wish. (I describe the dynamics of countertransference guilt in more detail on p. 52.) What holds for our patients is of course true for us as well: What is not represented consciously finds its expression through action (Freud, 1914g). In my experience working with and supervising other clinicians with chronically suicidal patients, actions related to an unconscious wish to abandon a patient come supported by clinical rationalizations. These include prematurely hospitalizing patients, abruptly referring them to another clinician, or using heavily sedating psychotropic medications. More subtle but equally concerning variations of these impulses occur in our everyday practices—forgetting to return phone calls or emails or, even more insidiously, not talking openly and directly with our patients about their suicidality for fear of what they might say. Defensive rationalizations may also include an exclusive focus on symptoms rather than feelings, efforts to control the patient's behavior (more on this below), or a denial about the seriousness of the patient's distress (Schechter et al., 2019).

Our unconscious guilt of wanting to abandon our patients can lead us in the opposite direction as well, masochistically enduring difficult treatments without important safeguards in place and not getting help from others when it is necessary for ourselves and our patients. What is crucial is to be able to face up honestly to what we are experiencing. By doing so, we give ourselves the opportunity to genuinely think through what would be helpful in the ever-fluctuating clinical moment.

## Countertransference cowardice

Stated bluntly, I was struggling with my cowardice and fantasies of not calling Brenda back. Although cowardice is certainly a loaded and pejorative term, I do feel it applies here. Countertransference cowardice is a topic we avoid talking about even with our most trusted supervisors. We seem to be more comfortable discussing actual and fantasied boundary violations (Celenza & Gabbard, 2003) and potential recklessness with heroic "unusual interventions" (Akhtar, 2018a) than discussing our wishes to shrink from our patients and their mental anguish. In his discussion of cowardice, Akhtar (2018b) describes physical, intellectual, and moral cowardice, respectively, all involving "a spontaneous reaction of helpless dread in the face of a massively traumatic situation" which leads to distress and inhibition (p. 375). What I am describing here are fantasies and experiences of *emotional cowardice* which lead us to want to flee situations that are frightening and feel unbearable for us to tolerate emotionally.

This term of course should not be used to chastise ourselves for feeling cowardice—we know as clinicians that persecutory self-attacks rarely lead to emotional growth or insight, either for us or for our patients. We should, however, take the time to really consider what we are dealing with when we treat suicidality. Any possibility of death or murder of a person we are becoming emotionally involved with will have consequences for us. Brenda could kill herself at any moment in our work together, and she often told me this bluntly. This is a horrific and helpless experience for us to endure that will inevitably lead to dread and hatred. Through projection of our fear and hatred, our suicidal patients can then feel menacing and even cruel. In their classic paper "Countertransference Hate in the Treatment of Suicidal Patients," Maltsberger and Buie (1974) conceptualize countertransference hatred towards suicidal patients as a mixture of aversion and sadism. They argue that because clinicians are more comfortable with aversion than with their sadistic fantasies, they are more likely when experiencing sadistic feelings to abandon the patient, thereby increasing the possibility of suicide:

> Suicidal crises are likely to arise when the torture is given up and withdrawal takes place [in the clinician] … there is a temptation to resort to abandonment of the patient in order not to acknowledge and bear, and place in perspective the countertransference malice. While the impulse to torment and torture will often be felt in some degree along with the impulse to abandon the relationship, in a great number of circumstances there is a reciprocal relationship between the intensity of the aversive impulse and the incapacity to tolerate conscious sadistic wishes. (p. 626)

This "aversive impulse" may be happening on a more global scale with our profession. As of 2018, suicide was the tenth leading cause of death overall in the United States and the second leading cause of death among individuals between the ages of ten and thirty-four. In 2019, 12 million adults aged eighteen or older reported having serious thoughts of suicide, and 1.4 million adults attempted suicide during the past year (NIMH website, 2021). Close to 800,000 people die by suicide every year around the world; that is, one person every forty seconds (WHO, 2021). These numbers are staggering and show no signs of remitting.

Many patients who suffer from suicidal thoughts and who do not respond to psychopharmacological or cognitive behavioral treatments will ask for our help, and we will need to face our wish to avoid them due to our dread of being with their unbearable suffering. Psychodynamic approaches to treating suicidal patients (Bateman & Fonagy, 2016; Clarkin et al., 1998) emphasize the important role of the therapist's countertransference but often do not highlight the potential emotional onslaught it can include.

## The angry formulation

Facing the prospect of calling Brenda back, I began anxiously reflecting on what was happening between us. Still in the midst of feeling dread, I noticed that my thoughts were leaning towards using psychoanalytic jargon and rigid diagnostic categories. Was Brenda, via projective identification due to her borderline personality organization, provocatively attempting to put her own hatred and desire to leave treatment in me because of her rage that I would abandon her? Was she again enacting a melancholic identification with her suicidal husband as a way of avoiding her own grief and trauma, leaving me in the position of feeling what she did when she found his dead body?

It seems to be commonplace that our first interpretations when we are experiencing dread with our patients are usually more about managing our own feelings than reflective of any true insight. While working on inpatient units with suicidal and traumatized patients with affective and psychotic symptoms, I noticed that clinicians (including myself) often used the term "borderline" or "acting out" spontaneously when a patient angered or frightened them. Grinberg's (1962) term "projective counteridentification" describes the violent use of "massive projective identification" by the patient to create a specific response in the analyst, who "is unconsciously and passively led to play the sort of role the patient hands over to him" (p. 436). Although Grinberg eloquently describes the feeling an analyst experiences in these situations, this feels too close to an "angry formulation" on the part of an analyst who is under immense psychic distress.

These "angry formulations" seem to serve the function of defensively reducing the dread that emerges in these often life-or-death situations by giving a false security of "knowing" what the patient is feeling or thinking. Implicitly these interpretations and diagnoses have a judgmental and persecutory quality reminiscent of the paranoid-schizoid position: Somebody is putting something inside us and we are passive victims from this attack on us. Casement (1985) refers to these types of interpretations as "cliché thinking." He argues that in moments of anxiety, the analyst applies psychoanalytic theory in a way that is sterile and stereotyped. This closes down opportunities for genuine experiences of discovery, for the analyst as well as the patient. A clue that this is happening is that curiosity and genuine interest in what is happening diminishes, and an attitude of rigidity emerges in our formulations that lead us away from our patient's experience and towards a more "textbook" explanation. Bolognini (2004) describes this phenomenon in terms of a "clever analyst." What a "clever analyst" cannot do is "to deal with what he observes in a creative way, in terms of psychoanalytic transformation, restitution and exchange. This lack of emotional contact with his own self turns him into an artist without paints: since he does not want to feel, he cannot make himself felt" (p. 76).

Bateman and Fonagy's (2016) concept of *hypermentalization* or *overactive pseudomentalizing* applies here as well in the countertransference experience of an "angry formulation." In contrast to an authentic and meaningful reflection on oneself and others in the process of mentalization, hypermentalization tends towards concrete and rigid thought processes that make one less receptive to new information and leans towards excessive and overly elaborated thinking about the mental states of others. In a hypermentalized state of mind, one's thinking about the mental states of others reflects their own individual biases and mental state rather than the actual experience of the other, and there is a trend towards constructing complex psychological explanations for interpersonal events that feel forced and inauthentic (Diamond et al., 2021).

## Guilt evasion and persecutory anxiety: Am I going to be sued?

Before I called Brenda back, another familiar dreadful idea occurred to me, of Brenda's committing suicide and my being held responsible for her death. What if her sons were to decide that it was my negligence that led to her dying? A vague but terrifying fantasy of being attacked and accused of being a perpetrator momentarily gripped me.

In my experience with supervision groups and with supervising psychotherapists, the fear of being sued is always present to some degree when clinicians work with patients who experience suicidal ideation. The fear of being sued is also behind rationalizations that many clinicians use to avoid treating patients who have attempted suicide in the past or who describe suicidal fantasies. Litigation is, of course, a real possibility. Fortunately, there are useful textbooks and guidelines describing current standards of care that ensure that one is providing the optimal level of care for at-risk patients (see Freedenthal, 2018; Shea, 2011). I would differentiate between, on one hand, the complicated realities of this clinical issue and the question of what is best practice and, on the other, the more primitive emotional state of dread about being punished and persecuted. This state involves unbearable countertransference guilt and its subsequent rage, which is projected and displaced as a terrifying persecutory fear of being punished and ruined.

For conceptual clarity, a broad definition of guilt is useful here. Guilt is difficult to define and describe precisely. It is usually about committing some crime or offense, either in reality or in fantasy. Although some authors label guilt, in contrast to shame, as a developmentally mature affective state (e.g., Tangney & Dearing, 2002), I regard guilt as distinct from shame (although one can feel both simultaneously) and see each as having its own developmental trajectory with a spectrum of primitive to mature variations (cf. Aron & Starr, 2013; Carveth, 2006). There is often a blurring between guilt and the subsequent fear of punishment, which are experienced together in more primitive forms of guilt (Wurmser, 2003). Klein (1948) observed that "persecutory guilt" is normally supplanted by "reparative guilt" on entry into the depressive/reparative position, where guilt then takes its more mature forms, including remorse and regret (Carveth, 2006).

An experience of dread occurs when one is not able to bear and name the imagined or real crime and the associated guilt, leading to a shift into a more primitive persecutory mode of being. This "guilt evasion" creates diffuse "doom and gloom" scenarios that feel menacing and persecutory—unconscious guilt undergoes externalization and gives rise to undue fears of adverse occurrences (Akhtar, 2013b; Jones, 1929;

Safán-Gerard, 2013). As a substitute for guilt, this unconscious need for punishment should not be conflated with the guilt it evades. What is necessary is facing up to guilt, understanding where it is coming from, and not confusing it with the experience of persecution. Carveth (2006) summarizes this eloquently:

> The challenge facing the guilt-evading subject is that of facing and bearing its guilt, integrating as a part of the tragic dimension of human existence the reality of our primordial ambivalence, and accepting as an aspect of "common human unhappiness" the need to shoulder the burden of responsibility to make reparation, and to change, which genuinely facing our guilt entails. Facing and bearing guilt opens the path toward restoration of a sense of inner goodness through reparative processes mediating identification with resurrected, surviving, comforting, forgiving, good internal objects. If advance in civilization entails an increased capacity to confront and bear guilt, then a first step may be to learn to speak its true language, not least by ceasing to confuse it with the self-torment that represents its evasion. (p. 194)

On reflection, my inability to bear my guilt before calling Brenda back led to fears of persecution that took the form of a fantasy of being sued and punished. Fueling my guilt was a fear of my own destructiveness and rage at Brenda for interrupting my peace of mind before a weekend and putting me into a helpless state of caring for her, an induced guilt related to my childhood history of feeling responsible and guilty for my own caregivers.

There was also a masochistic edge to my distress, in that being punished felt less uncomfortable than facing the guilt head-on. Racker (1968) notes that childhood conflicts such as these frequently lead one into a caregiver profession; to overcome or deny her guilt, the analyst tries to repair the childhood objects toward whom she felt aggression. When this project fails, the analyst is threatened with "the return of the catastrophe, the encounter with the destroyed object" (p. 174). A critical superego can perversely serve the function of protecting one from this depressive pain (Sedlak, 2019).

Our unawareness of or severe discomfort with our aggression and guilt will inadvertently be communicated to the patient by our tone of voice or other nonverbal cues. Instead of a genuine curiosity and respect for what our patient is experiencing, we may come across as critical and judgmental, or conversely overly sentimental and cloying. With a greater self-acceptance and curiosity about our full range of emotional reactions, there can be a more genuine and empathic attitude about what is happening between ourselves and our patients, and our emotional reactions can become more of an object of curiosity than "a dreaded sense of incontestable personal failing" (Sedlak, 2019, p. 59).

## Dread, manic defenses, and "empathism"

Brenda and I suffered through this episode and many others like it over the course of years working together. During this time, her suicidal thoughts and impulses lessened in frequency and intensity. This improvement seemed to be a result of our psychotherapy work together, some psychopharmacological interventions, and her deepening involvement with Alcoholics Anonymous and Narcotics Anonymous. In those communities she was able to find friendship and a language to describe her intense longing to magically rid herself of her mental pain and guilt over her husband's suicide via drugs, alcohol, and sexual activity. She also was able to talk with me about how the death of her husband resonated with her past trauma of losing her older brother to a drug overdose at the age of fourteen and her mother's subsequent depression and emotional withdrawal. It was a calm period in our work together—the dread felt like a distant memory.

Sadly, this tranquility collapsed shortly after the fifth anniversary of her husband's suicide. Brenda arrived at my office disheveled, hung over, and in tears about her recent breakup with a man with whom she was beginning to feel close. I felt a surge of a familiar sense of dread about the possibility of her committing suicide, a feeling I hoped I would not have to feel again. When I asked her about suicidal thoughts, she admitted to cutting herself with a razor in the shower, after drinking a bottle of wine, crying. "His dead body was with me … I could hear him telling me to just fucking die and end it."

Alarmed, I continued my questions in rapid succession, including asking her if she currently had any plans to hurt herself. She denied this and insisted that "it was the booze talking," noting that she had contacted her sponsor, Liz, who had talked with her at length and brought her to a meeting the morning after her relapse. "I feel better today, I guess. I'm okay." I immediately felt my dread diminish. I reflected that she had contacted her sponsor, reached out for help, gone to an AA meeting that morning, and was here now at her appointment. Maybe, I hoped, this was simply an anniversary reaction, and she would be able to reconstitute. These thoughts comforted me and lessened my dread. Brenda and I went over a detailed safety plan: She would stay with Liz for the next few days and go to AA or NA meetings daily, and we would meet again in two days. We discussed increasing the dose of her mood stabilizer medication and the possibility of an inpatient hospitalization, which she agreed to consider if her suicidal thoughts returned. I made sure Liz had no weapons or other implements Brenda could use to hurt herself. Brenda also said she was looking forward to seeing her son over the weekend. That session seemed to go quickly, and I felt relieved after she left.

I later got a call from her sponsor. Brenda had overdosed on her mood stabilizer while Liz was in the shower. In a panic, Liz had called 911, and Brenda was on her way to the emergency room. Shocked, I felt a feeling of vertigo and a sense of my world collapsing. It was an uncanny moment (Freud, 1919h) when what had felt familiar and safe with Brenda suddenly became unfamiliar and terrifying. A potent brew of helplessness, fear, anger, grief, guilt, and shame gripped me. How could I have missed this?

Thankfully, she survived the attempt. After she was discharged from the inpatient psychiatric hospital, we met in session and talked about what happened. Brenda told me she had anticipated all my questions and answered them the way she knew I wanted them answered. "You checked off all the right boxes, but you didn't seem to really get it. I was in pain," she told me bluntly.

Although her suicide attempt and my interventions could be interpreted in many ways, I want to focus on the truth of Brenda's words. A challenge for any clinician working with suicidal patients is the need to move flexibly between empathic listening and ongoing suicide risk assessment (Schechter et al., 2019). On reflection, I realized that in assessing her suicidality, I had subtly acted out a manic countertransference defense by her avoiding the emotional pain that felt unbearable for both of us—her anguish, grief, and rage that manifested themselves as a murderous destructiveness in the aftermath of her breakup with her lover.

Adapting the term "manic defense," originally proposed by Klein (1935) and later discussed as a countertransference by Racker (1968), I would formulate a countertransference manic defense against dread as the clinician's *wish for omnipotent control over the unbearable affective flooding involved in dread*. This is expressed in subtle or overt disparagement and denial of the patient's suffering, accompanied by an idealization of our abilities as clinicians to fix the situation by "doing something." This response favors action over receptivity; for example, quickly formulating a plan that makes sense to the therapist, who seeks to get compliance from the patient without noticing or attuning to what the patient is feeling during the process. The patient's overwhelming anguish and mental pain is bypassed, as is the clinician's guilt. As a result, the clinical severity of the situation is minimized with a plan for the patient that may be controlled and accomplished magically (Spillius et al., 2011). The outcome for the therapist is a sense of triumph, but for the patient is an empathic rupture.

Such ruptures can be missed by clinicians who are unconsciously attempting to manage their own dread. What occurs instead is *empathism*, an imitation of an empathic attitude that feels forced and superficial to our patients (Bolognini, 2004). Genuine empathy is a difficult and non-linear outcome of our attempt to engage and make deep contact with a wide range of our patients' emotional and psychic landscapes, their separateness, the complexity of their defenses, and their identifications with others. Empathy takes time and patience and is not the result of a forced "empathic attitude"—it is the product of a prolonged, disciplined, difficult effort toward deepening immersion with our patients and our growing awareness about what within us is getting in the way of this process. In his classic text on psychoanalytic empathy, Bolognini (2004) highlights the difference between empathy, a "structured receptivity" in the analyst, and empathism, noting:

> My concern instead is with the maintenance of a structured receptivity in the analyst and the reduction of his residual

narcissism and omnipotence, which might lead to empathism, in which the analyst strains by force to make contact at all costs, under the illusion of controlling the process better. (p. 133)

In supervision and in my own treatment, I began to face my difficulty with tolerating Brenda's dread. I was unconsciously enacting a relationship I felt as a child, feeling the dread of my family's intergenerational trauma of suicidality and my frantic desire to help her yet being powerless to do so. My dread was an expression of my inability to control Brenda and rid her of her immense psychic pain and suicidality, and my guilt was about my rage at her for putting me in the helpless position of being subject to her agony. As Bolognini (2004, p. 71) writes: "The analyst needs to have really worked through a deep mourning: mourning for the archaic omnipotent illusion that he can exert so much control over his own affects as to be able to decide what they have to be." I had to arrive at a new relationship to Brenda's most destructive and painful states of mind through my own internal work (Cooper, 2016). These insights helped me suffer with my dread in a new way, one that opened up more possibilities of being with Brenda without resorting to defensive attempts to avoid what either of us was feeling. Schneidman (1993) notes that suicide is best understood as a movement away from intolerable emotion, unendurable pain, or unacceptable anguish.

Over time, an insight that Brenda came to that felt helpful to her was that alarming me about her suicidality felt "like a drug." The moment she felt I was concerned and worried about her, she felt held and comforted, which soothed the pain of abandonment, isolation, and rage that she perpetually carried. My worry for her was what she wished she had received from her mother after her brother's death, and in the moment when she felt my dread, she momentarily found what she had longed for (only for it to be lost again).

# CHAPTER 4

# Erotic dread

*The analyst plays with fire! What brings about such madness?*
—Ellen Pinsky, 2017, p. 32

No writing on countertransference dread can be complete without attention to the dread of our own erotic desire in our work with patients. Central to any psychoanalytic therapy is our ability to be with intensity in all its forms, and sexuality and erotic fantasies cannot be anything but intense; being aroused, overstimulated, and anxious to some degree will inevitably be present in any intimate experience. Sexual feelings and passions are overwhelming and touch upon suffering; the suffering of pleasure, a "too muchness" of the excesses that the body and mind cannot contain or reach (Benjamin & Atlas, 2015). Gabbard's (1996) wonderfully honest description of struggling with an erotic enactment early in his career captures this dread:

> The already confining dimensions of my consulting room sud-
> denly seemed even smaller. My throat was dry and the pounding
> of my heart was palpable in my ears. I contemplated my options
> carefully. I could, of course, run out of the office screaming

(a course of action that seemed most in keeping with my affective state). I could be silent and mysterious in the same way my
analyst was with me. I could explain to her that her feelings were
a form of resistance to the therapy and tell her to stop having such
feelings. I could fake a nosebleed and tell her I'd be right back
after tending to it (that would at least buy some time to think).
I leaned back in my chair ... and I tried to look as thoughtful and
accepting as I could. (p. 1)

Facing and tolerating our experience of erotic dread without resorting
to seductive enactments or abandonments of our patients is a lifetime
struggle for all of us (Dalenberg, 2000). It is daunting to write about
this topic, however, in part because of the sheer amount that has already
been written by creative and thoughtful psychoanalysts; it is also true
that verbalizing our erotic feelings always feels too close to the act.
Talking about sex can never be devoid of a bodily experience. Atlas
(2015, p. 30) observes, "The movement between moments of sexual stim-
ulation and arousal to use of theory ... most papers tend to use words
as a way to regulate the reader and writer and protect from the erotic
through the use of distanced and 'professional' jargon." Sexuality simultaneously registers in the mind and body, act and desire (Stein, 2008).

## Erotic countertransference and the origins of the "talking cure"

In fact, erotic dread was probably experienced and enacted in the first
"talking cure," a term coined by Bertha Pappenheim (known by the
pseudonym "Anna O," a patient of Josef Breuer, who published her case
study in his book *Studies on Hysteria*, written with Freud) and who later
became a well-known feminist, writer, social pioneer, and the founder
of the *Jüdischer Frauenbund* (League of Jewish Women) (Kaplan,
1979). Although her treatment with Freud's mentor and collabora-
tor Josef Breuer is shrouded in misrepresentation and outright false-
hoods, it is clear from all accounts that Breuer was intensely devoted
to Pappenheim, seeing her often twice daily over two years, possibly
for over one thousand hours (Gilhooley, 2002), with Breuer writing,
"Her life became known to me to an extent to which one person's life is
seldom known to another" (Freud & Breuer, 1895d, pp. 21–22, quoted

in Gilhooley, 2002). Breuer frequently touched Pappenheim's hand, fed her, medicated her with opiates and sedatives, and at times forcibly restrained her (Gilhooley, 2002).

Breuer ended Pappenheim's treatment despite Pappenheim's worsening condition, and he appears to have remained traumatized by his experience of dread from this episode. Over two decades later, in a letter explaining to an enquirer why, after Anna O, he did not pursue an analytic method with his patients and instead referred them to Freud, he wrote: "… at that time learned a great deal—much that was of scientific value, but also the important practical lesson that it is impossible for a 'general practitioner' to treat such a case without his activity and the conduct of his life thereby being completely ruined. I vowed at the time never again to subject myself to such an ordeal" (Grubrich-Simitis, 1997, pp. 26–27, quoted in Britton, 1999).

Britton (1999, 2003) argues that this alleged erotic psychodrama, disclosed by Breuer privately to Freud, gave Freud the raw materials to theorize about a vast range of psychoanalytic concepts, including transference, countertransference, repetition compulsion, and acting out. Despite writing to Jung that an article "on 'counter-transference' is sorely needed" (quoted in McGuire, 1974, p. 475), Freud never wrote this article, and yet in his communication to Jung, he described erotic countertransference as "a permanent problem for us." His discomfort over the subject is clear, however, in the hypermasculine language he uses regarding the analyst's erotic feelings: The analyst needs to develop a "thick skin" to "dominate" the countertransference. In later writings, he described the importance of "overcoming" (1910d) the erotic countertransference and keeping it "in check" (1915a, p. 164).

Freud had good reason to be concerned. While he clearly understood and experienced the inevitability of erotic countertransference—he admitted to an unspecified "narrow escape" to Jung—he also witnessed its ruinous effects on his disciples and their patients. In the letter in question, Freud was addressing Jung's sexual involvement with his patient Sabina Spielrein, who later became a distinguished psychoanalyst. In their correspondence about her, both seem to cast blame on Spielrein for seducing Jung, and they implicitly downplayed the seriousness of what had occurred in her treatment. This tone contrasts with Freud's stern warnings in his published work about managing erotic transferences (Britton, 2003; Pinsky, 2017).

Clearly, developing a "thick skin" and "dominating" the erotic countertransference have not worked for us. Over a century later, sexual transgressions and boundary violations continue to haunt our profession (Celenza, 2007, 2014; Gabbard, 2017). As Blechner (2017) soberly notes, the list of psychoanalysts who have had sexual relationships with their patients, or married them, reads like a Who's Who of our field: Carl Jung, Sandor Ferenczi, Erich Fromm, Frieda Fromm-Reichmann, Wilhelm Reich, Otto Fenichel, Harry Stack Sullivan, Karen Horney, and many, many others. As analysts were acting out their sexual desires with patients and discussing the psychodynamics of their patients' sexual fantasies, there was a phobic dread of describing our own erotic experiences in the consulting room directly and openly, both in the literature and in consultations with each other (Davies, 1994; Tansey, 1994).

Over the past two decades, there has been a renewed interest and much courageous writing on our erotic countertransferences. Contemporary psychoanalytic theory downplays metaphors of a conquest over desire and instead emphasizes the importance of being able to do our best to mentalize, contain, and be curious about our erotic experiences. The literature is too vast to name here; my personal influences on this topic include Atlas (2015), Celenza (2014), Dalenberg (2000), Davies (1994), Gabbard (1996), Knafo and Bosco (2020), and McWilliams (1996). These authors, albeit with varying theoretical perspectives, all describe the early determinants of erotic transferences and countertransferences and the enigmatic sexual unconscious always present in human relations and in our fantasy life; they emphasize the universal desire for bodily contact, arousal, and merger that are inherent in all intimate human relationships, including between analyst and analysand. This is of course no easy task for the analyst to bear. Pinsky (2017) sums this up well:

> The enterprise is full of paradoxes and contradictions: the situation is real, it's unreal; it's staged, it's real life; it's personal; it's impersonal; it's theoretical; it's an artifice; it's not artificial; it starts with "no," it stirs up "yes"; it provides safeties, these safeties heat things up; it frustrates, it relaxes; it forbids, it permits; if it succeeds, it disappoints (try saying that about your orthopedic surgery); "psychoanalytic treatment is founded on truthfulness" but it begins with a seduction; it's founded on truthfulness but

self deception is fundamental to being human … what will pre-
pare the analyst for such an "impossible profession"? (p. 36)

The analyst's receptivity to the struggle inherent in these "impossible"
circumstances opens up possibilities of psychic transformation and
growth for patients and analysts alike (Celenza, 2014). Where there is
possibility, however, there is danger and dread as well. Britton (2003)
rightly warns that there are no tame tigers, and that animal trainers and
zookeepers need to be the first to realize the dangers inherent in working with these primal forces.

## Variations of erotic countertransference dread

Erotic countertransference dread can take many forms. Moments of
dread laced with shame and guilt can surge even in the simple act of
experiencing erotic feelings or fantasies about a patient. Patients disclosing their sexual fantasies and erotic desires towards the analyst can
cause dread and obsessional anxiety about how to handle these vulnerable moments in treatment (Dalenberg, 2000). More overt and frightening experiences of dread occur when a patient's sexual transferences
have predatory and aggressive components or when they are expressed
in a regressed erotized transference. Both experiences, on the part of
both the patient and analyst, may be defenses against more primal and
shameful fantasies of merger and dependency (Balint, 1968; Blum, 1973;
Celenza, 2014; Kernberg, 1994).

I want to focus here on a more insidious form of erotic dread—the
dread of experiencing the full range of our sexual and gender fluidity,
with all of the erotic and sensual aspects this involves. Despite Freud's
(1905d) insistence that we all are polymorphously stimulated and bisexual in our erotic fantasy life, much of the psychoanalytic literature on
erotic countertransferences is cast in a heteronormative paradigm, dis-
avowing and pathologizing individuals who do not conform to these
standards. This rigidity has caused irreparable harm to individuals and
communities outside these categories, a phenomenon that has been well
documented elsewhere (Abelove, 2016).

Another consequence has been a narrowing of analysts' abilities to feel the full range of their own erotic experience. As both

Gabbard (1996) and Celenza (2014) note, there is an unfortunate tendency in psychoanalytic theorizing to generalize about the nature of the transference and countertransference based on the gender and sexual orientation of patient and analyst. Most analysts are more comfortable when their erotic countertransference matches their conscious gender and sexual identities (Hirsch, 1993; Shapiro, 1993).

In reality, there is considerable gender and sexual fluidity in the roles played by both analyst and patient in the analytic drama, and if these are allowed to emerge without premature foreclosure, a variety of transferences and countertransferences emerge that involve homosexual, heterosexual, and pansexual longings—not being an "either/or," but a "both/and"; the "two and the many" (Celenza, 2014). Accessing these feelings can cause significant disruptions in the analyst, which can lead to a more rigid and sterile experience for the patient and analyst alike. Patraka's (1992) term "binary terror" captures the dread faced when blurring of boundaries between binaries that have been integral to a culture's social discourse are threatened. Our defenses against this terror can lead to enactments as described below.

## Case example

Sujata was a twenty-six-year-old graduate student in comparative literature who developed an interest in psychoanalysis after reading Freud and Kristeva in graduate seminars. She was especially interested in the intersections of gender, semiotics, sexuality, and trauma. Sujata identified as a trans woman and was meticulous about her appearance—I experienced her as strikingly attractive, with a dignified presence that felt slightly emotionally distant.

Privately, Sujata expressed doubts about her gender and sexuality, finding herself at times imagining herself as a boy, and sometimes feeling neither masculine nor feminine, only "fat and ugly." She was attracted to both men and women but had sexual experiences with only women and gender nonbinary partners. Sujata had grown up in a Bangladeshi family, an only child to her first-generation immigrant parents, who owned a retail business. Born biologically male, she identified as female as a young child. She described a childhood of isolation, shame, and continual conflict with her parents, who alternated between being alarmed, perplexed, horrified, and angry at Sujata for identifying as female. She described her mother as "totally clueless and hysterical" about these issues and her father as quietly enraged and emotionally distanced about her transitioning.

Isolated from her family and her classmates, Sujata found solace in multiple online communities who introduced her to poets, authors, and philosophers versed in queer theory and narratives, which inspired her early successes as a writer. Unfortunately, her online presence subjected her to several sexual assaults and predatory behavior which continued to traumatize her.

Sujata began her analysis eagerly and took to the task as an earnest student, freely associating and talking about her gender, sexuality, and her traumatic upbringing, often in rapid succession. She would refer to Marx, continental theory, Lacan, and trauma studies, often leaving me scrambling just to keep up with her and to figure out what she was saying. I was awed and intimidated by her brilliance, but I was also often left frustrated and confused after our sessions. Over the first year, I found myself struggling in trying to help her make connections between her past, the pain she was carrying, and the ways she avoided uncomfortable feelings with me. She seemed to agree with what I had to say, but it felt as if there was an impenetrable barrier of theory and intellectualization between us.

A shift occurred about a year into our work together. After one of our sessions, I walked out of the office to go to the bathroom, and suddenly Sujata emerged out of the women's room, our bodies running into each other. Caught off guard, I felt a surge of dread and shame. Sujata appeared momentarily visibly surprised and then gave me a nervous smile and laugh and walked away.

For reasons that were at first unclear to me, I was shaken by the experience. Although nothing untoward had occurred, the dread I felt suggested an act that was forbidden and intimate. This uncomfortable closeness felt in stark contrast to the emotional distance we usually had with one another. I realized that despite my overtly neutral affirming stance towards her gender and sexuality, implicitly I was uncomfortable with my own interest and desire to get closer to her. This discomfort was a complicated brew of attraction, curiosity, and envy of her body. Instead of feeling through my experience with Sujata in an intimate and sensual way, I was trying to "figure her out" to make sense of my inchoate desires. Although we often spoke about her gender and sexuality, I was not participating with her in an embodied and authentic way—I had been treating her gender and sexuality as facts, not as areas of delight or genuine curiosity.

These insights offered me more freedom to talk playfully with her about the awkwardness of the bathroom situation and her experience of being with me in the office. With an ironic smile, she said she had a suspicion that I was more like her father than I thought I was; a cis-gendered heterosexual Indian man who was kind of clueless and silently judgmental about her sexuality and gender. These were some of the first authentic moments we shared together about how she was experiencing our relationship. Later in the analysis, she began to recognize that her compulsive need to intellectualize was a way of coping with the loss of her mother's bodily affection and tenderness. Allowing herself to feel feminine was both liberating and dangerous, in part because it signi-fied the loss of her mother's affectionate touching, caressing, and hold-ing that she longed for and had felt when she had been her mother's cherished little boy.

## Maternal erotic countertransferences

My dread of experiencing sexual and gender fluidity with Sujata led me to a distanced paternal enactment, which was a defensive distanc-ing from a more affectionate and tender maternal erotic closeness. In a child's development, the erotic is there from the moment of birth in every cuddle, tickle, diaper change, and feeding. Through these intimate acts, the infant's body and mind become libidinized, through caregiv-ers' careful, mostly unconsciously titrated balance between under- and overstimulation (Davies, 2013). To break through our mutual intellec-tualizing defenses, my dread of the undercurrent of our erotic closeness needed to be faced. McWilliams (1996) writes,

> A genuinely empathic stance requires more than the intellec-tual "admission" of polymorphous trends; it requires that the therapist be able to feel and enjoy them. It further requires a capacity to appreciate and even envy the positive, joyful aspects of participation ... a paradox of working sensitively across a

sexual-orientation gap, then, is that one must appreciate simultaneously both individual psychological particularity and universal
sexual omnivorousness. (p. 210)

Some of the origins of my erotic dread with Sujata had to do with my
experiencing more primal and early countertransferences related to my
mother's body (Celenza, 2014). Welles and Wrye (1991) describe how
the maternal erotic countertransference may be highly disconcerting
to the analyst. Both analyst and patient may experience simultaneous
terror of and longing for fusion, which can include boundary diffusion
and loss of separate gender identity. These include sensual bodily fantasies that involve "messing, smearing, poking, exposing, getting inside,
pouring, patting, and making" (p. 673 ). Kumin (1985) used the term
"erotic horror" to describe how to convey the terror of a similar experience, involving a sexually exciting but frustrating past object relationship revealing itself in dissonant gender configurations in the analytic
dyad. Kristeva (1982) notes Freud's emphasis on castration anxiety over
the "dread of incest" which forces a "confrontation with the feminine" as
a taboo (p. 59). All these components of an archaic maternal countertransference can lead to erotic dread.

In conclusion, as opposed to "conquering" our erotic countertransference, I have tried to stress here the importance of allowing ourselves to
face our dread of feeling the full range of our sexual and erotic life in all
of its forms. McWilliams (1996) wisely notes that analysts should experience "remnants of fetishes; pleasure in exhibitionistic and voyeuristic
ideas; fantasies of being the other sex or both sexes at once; experiences
of feeling like an infant, child, adolescent, adult, parent; images of domi-
nance and submission, sadism and masochism, blissful merger, raging
omnipotence, and every other variant of sexualized appetite in which
humanity has dabbled" (p. 210). Here the emphasis is not on translation
or rational understanding as an end in itself; it is on the analyst's ability
to participate in the rhythms of the patient's experience and suffering,
allowing for a relational home for the experience itself (Cooper, 2016;
Reis, 2020; Spezzano, 2007). To do this, we must let go of our wish to
conquer our countertransference and have the courage to be with what
feels unbearable.

# CHAPTER 5

# Dissociation

*Whoever fights monsters should see to it that in the process he does not become a monster. And if you gaze long enough into an abyss, the abyss will gaze back into you.*

—Friedrich Nietzsche

As clinicians, we value the necessity of our patients being able to share what before tormented them in isolation. This often requires an emotional and somatic immersion in their inner torment that reaches the primitive layers of *our own* personal experiences of trauma; a "too muchness" signified by an intensity that resonates with our patient's lived experience in profound and disturbing ways. There are of course no "trigger warnings" for what emerges in the lived moment with our patients in the consulting room. Bearing witness to the unimaginable and unbearable aspects of human existence—including cruelty, death, violence, torture, incest, profound neglect—hurls us into the eternal struggles between living and dying, *eros* and *thanatos*. A wish to reach out despite the vulnerability and pain and do our best to "love life" is in perpetual conflict with the pull towards nothingness, annihilation, and ultimately death and dedifferentiation (Reis, 2011). There often is no place to hide or escape in this intimate and disturbing relatedness.

With no clear way out, we resort to other means to escape. Dissociation is our last-resort survival strategy, the escape when there is no escape (Putnam, 1997; Schore, 2019). "Dissociation" (from the Latin *dis* ["apart"] and *sociare* ["join together"]) was originally used in early fifteenth-century science to depict the point when a breakdown of elements occurs in a chemical reaction. Subsequently, it was used to describe individuals who are "separated from companionship" or have left their group (Moskowitz et al., 2019). The psychological use of the term is metaphorical and leans on these original meanings: "dis-associating" involves making and keeping apart what would normally be connected. Definitions of dissociation have ranged from being a healthy and useful capacity of the mind to focus attention and engage in deep states of absorption, to a pathological response to unbearable mental pain and trauma (Howell, 2020).

## Dissociation: a process or a structure?

Pathological and defensive variations of dissociative experiences have had multiple and overlapping definitions, from a broad, more process-oriented definition to narrower, structural concepts (Howell, 2020; Moskowitz et al., 2019). *Process*-oriented definitions involve alterations in consciousness that keep apart aspects of subjectivity that would otherwise be connected or unified. Examples include a whole range of experiencing, including altered hypnotic or trance states, narrowing awareness, selective absorption, psychic numbing, and alienation from one's body (Blum, 2013; Howell, 2005, 2020). These alterations in consciousness often reflect a more primary mind-body detachment within the self, which unlinks one from the rhythms and tempo of embodiment—in this sense, dissociation can be seen as a way of regulating, moment by moment, the degree of the "psyche's embeddedness in the sensorial and temporal life of the body" (P. Goldberg, 2020). It should be noted, however, that there are significant disagreements about the nature of dissociative processes, with some authors conceptualizing dissociation as a "neural reflex" due to trauma and separating the term from more commonplace hypnoid phenomena (Purcell, 2020) and others emphasizing the role of dissociative processes as a defensive prevention of symbolization due to trauma (Diamond, 2020).

A narrower *structural* definition of dissociation refers to ways in which trauma renders emotion, thought, and memory inaccessible to each other and to the rest of the self, thereby creating separate self-states (Nijenhuis & Van der Hart, 2011). In contrast to repression, however, which usually involves symbolized fantasies that have some narrative coherence which have been rendered unconscious due to intrapsychic conflict, dissociation involves split off, fragmentary, poorly symbolized elements that have a lack of narrative coherence, often due to unbearable psychic pain and trauma (Busch et al., 2021). Contemporary relational psychoanalysis views dissociation and multiplicity as a normal process that facilitates adaptation and creativity, which is then enlisted as a defense against unbearable developmental trauma by creating multiple, structuralized states of mind (Bromberg, 2003). These dissociative "not me" states (Bromberg, 1996; D. B. Stern, 2004, 2009; Sullivan, 1953) can have powerful hidden effects on thought and behavior. Traumatic dissociation speaks to the mandate not to know, a mandate that requires one to split off parts of self and self-experience to avoid the integration of feelings, memories, and bodily sensations (Pearlman & Saakvitne, 1995).

In this chapter, to broaden awareness of dissociative experiences that could otherwise go unrecognized in clinicians, I treat dissociation as both process and structure. In particular, I will highlight ways in which pathological dissociative processes and structures in us go unrecognized and have profound effects on our patients. These forms of dissociation transform our lived and embodied experience of being with our patients into gradations of an "undead" experience—inhabiting deadness as if it were aliveness (Reis, 2011). Countertransference dissociation defined this way is the disruption in the continuity of mental experience for the purposes of warding off the unbearable experiences we encounter clinically and cannot escape (Auchincloss & Samberg, 2012; Pearlman & Saakvitne, 1995).

## Dissociation dissociated from psychoanalysis

There are historical roots to neglect of our dissociative states of mind. Psychoanalysis has a fraught history with the concept of dissociation. Even though Freud was originally interested in it (in his writing about "hypnoid states" in hysteria, consequent to sexual trauma), after he developed his ideas about repression and structural theory, he alluded to dissociation only indirectly (I. Brenner, 2009; Kluft, 1996). Freud's (1936a) last words on the subject of "split personality" spoke to his discomfort:

> Depersonalization leads us on to the extraordinary condition of "double conscience" which is more correctly described as "split personality." But all of this is so obscure and been so little mastered scientifically that I must refrain from talking about it any more to you. (Freud, quoted in Brenner, 2009, p. 57)

Freud's uncertainty may reflect his eventual alienation from his colleague Sandor Ferenczi, who prioritized trauma (Hainer, 2016) and his competition with his contemporary, Pierre Janet, who was a pioneer in describing dissociation and its relationship to trauma. In contrast to their work, Freud's models did not speak to the fluctuations and variations in consciousness that are characteristic of dissociation (Van der Hart, 2016).

Sexism is also a factor in the former psychoanalytic deafness to dissociation. Women with dissociative symptoms and sexual trauma were (and still are) pathologized, ridiculed, or flatly disbelieved. Men often hide their dissociative processes in isolation of affect, negation of their bodies, hyper-rationality, and various forms of emotional stonewalling and schizoid retreats under the mask of "reason."

Elizabeth Severn, whom Freud infamously called "an evil genius" because of her influence on Ferenczi, suffered from sexual trauma and dissociative symptoms and has only recently been recognized for her innovative contributions to psychoanalytic theory (Rachman, 2018). The stigma of dissociation continues to this day, with talented clinicians often feeling shame about disclosing dissociative experiences to colleagues and supervisors. This reluctance may be due in part to the universal need to negate or minimize the profound effects of trauma, especially incest and childhood sexual trauma (Herman, 1992; McWilliams, 2011; Pearlman & Saakvitne, 1995). Considering the high rates of early sexual abuse and sexual assault in the general population (Finkelhor, 2019; Finkelhor et al., 2014) and the ubiquity of developmental trauma and its relationship to dissociation, it seems clear that trauma and dissociation do not reside only in our patients—we must face our own traumas and moments of deadness as well. Elizabeth Howell describes the clinical dyad as a "wounded dyad": to varying degrees we are all traumatized and dissociative, and as therapists we must honestly recognize, metabolize, and deal with our own blind spots and traumas (Howell, 2020).

## The hidden dissociation of everyday clinical experience

Our immersion in the therapeutic situation involves an oscillation of various forms of consciousness within our own bodies and our inter-subjective presence; in our daily flow of experience with patients, one can notice a variety of subtle and not-so-subtle, acute and chronic, dissociative responses in ourselves. Intimately connected with trauma, dissociation is often hidden, shame-ridden, and hard to see—in others and especially in ourselves. It can create a blank space in memory and attention that goes unrecognized—we cannot know what we do not know or remember what we do not remember (Chefetz, 2015; Howell, 2020). There can be a kind of complacent "going on being," a false sense of coherence that misses what is being dissociated. As Chefetz (2015) notes,

> Dissociation is not a banishing act ... it is a paradoxical binding-disruption where the tag ends of what ought to match can't connect. They are held in close proximity, tethered but outside awareness ... we all seek coherence ... through whatever mode of expression will finally, logically and emotionally make sense out of what was incoherent, unbearable, and unspeakable. (p. 52)

Dissociative processes are not kept secret or disguised; they simply go unnoticed, shifting the attention away from rifts in the self, masking its disunity, allowing a fiction of a stable unity (P. Goldberg, 2020). We may allude to a dissociative process when we use vague language to describe internal deadness. To say one is "burned out," "worn out," "out of it," "checked out," "spaced out," "empty," "numb," "done," "drained," or "tapped out" is to speak the language of dissociative processes in our everyday experience with patients and our body awareness; the fluctuations in consciousness we inhabit to manage carrying unbearable emotional pain. Underneath these words is an experience of feeling a loss of vitality, feeling "undead," and a sense of not fully being in our bodies or with our patients.

Therapists who work with trauma survivors have recognized countertransference dissociation for decades. Dissociative experiences in witnesses to trauma have been described by concepts such as "secondary traumatization" (Bloom, 1997), "contact victimization" (Courtois, 1988), "compassion fatigue" (Figley, 1995), and "traumatic countertransference" (Dalenberg, 2000; Herman, 1992). In a groundbreaking work, Pearlman and Saakvtine used the term "vicarious traumatization" for the impact of dissociative countertransference experiences in acute moments in treatment as well as for more chronic effects of trauma-witnessing (McCann & Pearlman, 1990; Pearlman & Saakvitne, 1995).

Pearlman and Saakvtine (1995) explore therapists' use of dissociation to manage intense effects and traumatic material, construing this experience as a normal part of working with trauma and observing that it happens with high frequency. They urge us to be aware of these reactions, as they are easily overlooked because of the therapist's shame and/or personal history of trauma. More recent contributions in the relational psychoanalytic literature use the term "counter-trauma" to capture the complex interweaving of trauma and dissociation in the "fluid, intersubjective, two-person" field in which therapist and patient participate (Gartner, 2014). All these contributions frame countertransference dissociation as simultaneously vital and unwelcome.

## Case example

As a psychiatric resident on call, I remember being asked around 2 a.m. to see a young woman in the throes of a psychotic episode, visibly pregnant in her third trimester. I could hear her screaming as I was walking towards the locked inpatient unit. The nurses and techs had her in seclusion in a padded room and were visibly shaken, surrounding her, trying to calm her down. She was pacing, furiously screaming, and punching the walls. "We need meds, Doc, give this girl some meds!" the nurse holding her down pleaded. The woman's face was in deep agony with fury and pain. I approached her gently to speak to her and she spat in my face. "Fuck you—no! Don't touch me, get away from me!" she screamed.

"Just give her meds, Doc, don't talk to her!" the nurse yelled. I felt a surge of panic and then found myself unable to concentrate. A kind of stupor fell over me. I wanted to do whatever I could to make "the situation" go away, to have her "go away." In that moment, she was no longer a person I was with, she was a terrible menace from which I wanted to get away.

It was an especially difficult week for me in the inpatient unit. One of my patients, a woman with a lifelong history of sexual trauma, attempted to strangle herself with her sleep apnea machine. Another fainted and fell out of her shower due to low blood pressure from her antipsychotic, a medication I had prescribed. A mother of a patient on the unit screamed at me at a family meeting for holding their daughter on the unit longer than expected. I remember walking out of the hospital stunned and numb. A concerned friend urged me to engage in "self-care": take a walk in nature, do something pleasurable and meaningful, and so on. But all I wanted to do was find a way to be less alive. I wanted to drink bourbon, smoke a cigarette, and watch mindless television. I felt a need to deaden myself to avoid a collapse I felt was bottomless.

About fifteen years later, I am sitting with Helen, an intimidating sixty-six-year-old survivor of incest and profound neglect. Images and memories of my experiences that week in residency suddenly enter my consciousness, taking me by surprise. The agony in the pregnant woman's eyes and her rage towards me rise to the surface, distracting me from what Helen is saying. Helen and I have been working together for three years. She has a lot to say—it is often difficult to keep up with her. A successful attorney, she is an expert at using language, but there is often a lack of a felt sense of what her words are about. Our sessions feel like an onslaught of verbiage intended to avoid any awareness of our being together in the present moment. Helen lives alone and does not have children. She often speaks of a profound sense of being isolated from life and from others around her, and has a difficult time understanding why colleagues and acquaintances fail to call her back or seem not to want to know her better.

While Helen is rapidly recounting the minutia of her day at the office, I find myself trying to validate what she is saying, doing my best to be empathic, while another part of me is remembering that week in residency. A hollow feeling gnaws at me. I am doing my best to be present, but I can't focus on, or really remember, Helen's words. My body feels paradoxically heavy yet absent. Realizing I am distracted, rousing myself, I begin to wonder why I was thinking about that week in residency. Were these thoughts about the past a reverie (Ogden, 1997) that spoke to something in Helen's experience, a way she was communicating feelings of anguish and sorrow underneath her empty speech about her day? These efforts at thinking felt hazy and sluggish, and there was a continued absence of sensations in my body. Towards the end of the session, I say, "I wonder if underneath all of what you are saying is genuine sadness and helplessness that's difficult to talk about with me, so you instead focus on other topics to distract yourself." The words felt empty and lifeless as I said them, but I felt I had to offer something.

"I guess so, that makes sense," Helen says, and keeps talking, not missing a beat. As she leaves the office, she turns to me and says, "I'm tired all the time and I don't feel anything is really changing or going anywhere." I feel tired as well, and in a kind of stupor. I am relieved the session is over, but I have a sense of having missed something important. Is this analysis going anywhere?

At our session the next day, Helen begins in her characteristic way, talking rapidly about her day and describing feeling isolated. Suddenly, she pauses and says, "I need to ask you something." I suddenly feel nervous and exposed, as if I have also been anticipating this confrontation. "Yesterday you seemed checked out, in fact I feel like you've been checked out now over the past couple of weeks. I'm not sure why or what's going on with you, but you are starting to remind me of those robot therapists they talk about on the news. You know, the ones you can program to parrot back what you say if you're pathetic and alone. *Yes, Helen, that must be difficult for you, tell me more!* It's therapy-talk for dummies. Are you even alive?"

I suddenly feel defensive—the urge to counter her criticisms and hostility take the form of a rising abdominal tension, a somatic jolt felt in my body of wanting to attack Helen back and defend myself. Although I could not have formulated this at the time, I want to make Helen's way of being with me the problem, the reason for my being "checked out." She constantly keeps me at a distance, and now it's *my* fault? Resurrected from my undead experience with Helen, I suddenly felt the quickening pulse and heat of my anger towards her—I certainly feel alive now, alive in my rage.

Back in touch with my body and my anger towards Helen, I realized I was "checked out" for much of our last week together. I had attributed my "reverie" about my residency to some form of unconscious communication from Helen. I feel I made an error here that therapists make when we are not fully present with our patients; assuming that what I was thinking about had meaning for her and focusing on the cognitive *content* of my intrusive memory as a way of trying to understand her, as opposed to the *process* of what I was experiencing in the flow of the session with her—my inability to be present with Helen's subjective reality (Eshel, 2019).

Reflecting on it now, my memories of what I went through during residency probably represented a communication from my unconscious about how *I* felt with Helen: helpless, anguished, enraged, and unable to reach her; identifying with my past self as a resident as well as the pregnant woman in a furious state of agony and rage. These images, shorn of any bodily awareness or somatic embodiment, were emblematic of how I was dissociated from Helen's experience of trauma, as I had been with the pregnant woman. Writing this, it feels important to mention that I do not remember the pregnant woman's name or anything about her that felt relationally meaningful, just the experience of what happened to me in her fit of rage and psychic pain. With some shame, I realized I had been emotionally absent from Helen in a similar way.

## Dissociation and attunement

Helen was attuned to my misattunement, my inability to be present and alive in her lived experience. Although I had the appearance of being there, I was not really "there" with her as an embodied presence. Freud (1912e) famously wrote that the technique of psychoanalytic listening "is a very simple one … It consists in not directing one's notice to anything in particular and in maintaining the same 'evenly suspended attention' in the face of all that one hears." He recommended that the analyst "should withhold all conscious influences from his capacity to attend, and give himself over completely to his unconscious memory" (pp. 111–112). This "very simple" attentional technique turned out to be not so simple after all, considering the countless subsequent papers on this putatively easy way to listen to patients.

One common thread that is known to all of us is a need for the analyst to have an open, receptive stance without resorting to intellectual or rational ways of listening to the patient. Theodor Reik (1948) wrote of the unconscious process by which the analyst deciphers the patient's unconscious dynamics, which he called "listening with the third ear." This process has a nonverbal, melodic character that assimilates the affective nuances of unconscious mentation: "Sounds, fleeing images, organic sensations, and emotional currents are not yet differentiated" (p. 9).

More recent psychoanalytic theorizing places emphasis on the relational, somatic, and intersubjective nature of attunement. Attunement is recognized as a kinesthetic and sensory awareness of an implicit understanding that is nonlinear and bidirectional. Good clinicians resonate like tuning forks to a variety of emotional pitches and to the nuanced shifting of emotional tone (Hopenwasser, 2008).

Contemporary analytic theory describes this as a reciprocal, mutually regulated process that can expand states of consciousness in both parties. These are the often subtle but meaningful affective happenings that unfold in moments from second to second in the clinical moment (Abbasi, 2018; D. N. Stern, 2004). Markman (2020) describes the analyst's embodied attunement within a unique relationship of two bodies together and the interpersonal rhythm of cadence, tone intensity, and movement that is generated by the participation of both analyst and analysand. Patients sense our presence and availability in this interpersonal rhythm, which is the "pulse" of the relationship which directs our interventions (Markman, 2020).

Using evocative metaphors of jazz and dance, Knoblauch (2020) describes the uncertainty, multiplicity, and vulnerability in the embodied flow of the clinical process as a *polyrhythmic weave*, a movement with multiple rhythms, pauses, and punctuations between the patient and analyst. Attention to this embodied process provides the analyst with an expanded awareness of subtle registered signals and enacted communications in the face of dissociation and moments of retreat and retaliation by either the patient or analyst. This complex intersubjective process is fluid, and not yet fully formulated or symbolized. It shapes the encounter on nonsymbolic, embodied registers of affect that can gradually allow for more finely tuned and complexly intertwined meanings to emerge in the process.

## Mind–body dissociation

Contemporary psychoanalysts also emphasize the role of being attuned to our bodies in our lived experience with our patients. As stated above, being able to *rationally think* about what is happening in the therapeutic encounter often misses the importance of fluctuations in states of consciousness in *being* with patients; our ability to be authentic, attuned, and somatically receptive to a range of affective and somatic states received from our patients and our own bodies. In fact, we come to know ourselves and our world through our bodily experiences; our bodies in contact with the world and others (Sletvold, 2014).

Cognitive processes dissociated from our bodily awareness and a felt sense of being with patients can lead to countertransference blunders with profound negative effects on the therapeutic process. In a series of important and clinically useful writings on body–mind dissociation in psychoanalysis, Lombardi (2002, 2008, 2009, 2017) describes body–mind dissociation as a situation in which the body exists concretely but disappears from lived experience; what is lost is the body experienced as the container for all of our subjective experience. The natural progression and interweaving of body, affect, and thought is dissociated; thinking is used to avoid the experience of sensations and bodily awareness, which is feared to be catastrophic and unbearable (Lombardi, 2009). Thinking then reaches into infinity, evading the reality of our lived experience with the limitations of our bodies and time. Lombardi notes that we often move towards interpersonal and transference-based interpretations to avoid our own subjective experiencing of our bodies and the felt bodily experience of our patients, insisting that "… the analyst must operate on the same unorganized levels of fluid, untranslatable and potentially explosive sensations that the analysand is living through" (2017, p. 34).

At these primitive levels, the analyst is confronted with *somatic countertransferences*, which are transferences into the analyst's own body, so that the analyst's body functions like a receptor organ for the analysand's unconscious communications. The whole body becomes a sort of "tympanic membrane" for receiving purposes (Lombardi, 2017, p. 35). Beyond our conscious intentions, the experiences we have with our patients accompany us continuously, often in dissociated splits between our bodies and our ways of thinking. Accessing these somatic memory traces and finding ways of translating what presents in the body as pre-representable or minimally represented into a psychically figurable form is the task of our working through our dissociative countertransferences (Botella & Botella, 2005; Diamond, 2020).

My lack of bodily awareness and sluggishness with Helen led to a defensive cognitive scrambling for understanding in the form of a false reverie; in retrospect these intellectualizations helped me stay feeling alive and dead simultaneously, thereby avoiding a more intimate bodily encounter with the archaic and unbearable aspects of Helen's anguish and trauma. Peter Goldberg (2020) importantly notes, however, that countertransference reactions to dissociative experiences in the analyst should not be assumed to reflect a patient's unconscious life; instead, they could also be the "analyst's singular and lonely response to deprivation" of true contact with the patient (p. 783).

Taking into account these fluctuations in our embodied attunement with patients, two forms of countertransference dissociation can be described, a micro-level "moment" of dissociation, and more chronic, macro-level forms of dissociative experience (Cavelzani & Tronick, 2016). With Helen, both were happening, in multiple overlapping ways.

## Micro-level acute dissociation

Micro-level countertransference dissociations are acute, often sudden dissociative moments that interrupt our ability to reflect on our own embodied emotional states, leading to an immediate emphasis on experience-distant cognitions and intellectualizations. My words spoken to Helen at the end of the session felt lifeless because they were said from a dissociated voice, one that was disembodied from the moment, more intellectual than lived-in. This lack of implicit mentalizing during such moments creates shifts in our tone of voice, gestures, and body posture to which the patient is attuned, and to which he may respond implicitly, as Helen did. Affective immediacy is blunted, and the patient can sense viscerally our lack of attunement.

Experientially, micro-level moments of dissociation in the counter-transference involve psychic numbing, avoidance, and a diminished range of affect—a "glazed over" quality of experience with a warped perception of time and a numbing of bodily sensations. I felt all these with Helen. Such acute dissociative moments occurred when she spoke in a rapid, atonal, disembodied manner, and when her thought process veered towards being overly inclusive of details about her day. In hindsight, such countertransference dissociations often occurred as Helen was approaching emotionally charged material that she could not tolerate, usually involving her experiences of sexual violence.

Being emotionally honest about these experiences is difficult. Professional literature mentions moments of fatigue, boredom, memory lapses, and distortions in time (Bollas, 1983; I. Brenner, 2004; Chefetz, 2009; Schmithusen, 2012). Bionian concepts such as "attacks on linking" and the "Beta screen" speak to ways the analyst's mind can be overwhelmed by traumatic material, leading to psychic paralysis. Bion describes having "the experience of being sleepy but not being able to fall asleep … at the same time of not being able to stay awake either as though both states, sleep and that of being awake, were interfered with by elements from the other state" (quoted in Symington & Symington, 1996, p. 65).

Recent psychoanalytic theorizing directly names dissociation as an essential element in our countertransference experience, especially when we work with patients who dissociate actively in sessions (I. Brenner, 2004; Chefetz, 2009; Eshel, 2019; Gabbard, 2014; McWilliams, 2011; Newirth, 2016; Pearlman & Saakvitne, 1995). The traumatized patient's uses of auto-hypnotic defenses and projective identification have been highlighted as central aspects of this countertransference experience. Hopenwasser (2008) uses the paradoxical term "dissociative attunement" to emphasize the value of attending to our dissociative experiences with patients, as we may thus attain implicit knowledge that may not be available to conscious awareness.

Eshel (2019) describes what this is like experientially for the therapist:

> After ten or fifteen minutes, my laborious attentiveness would gradually diminish, and I would become detached. It was not that my thoughts wandered or that I was bored. Nothing. Blank. Absent. I ceased to exist as a person who listened, thought, and responded. I would sometimes become numb and sleepy. (p. 70)

Several caveats are worth noting here, however. Boredom and various forms of fatigue in an analytic session do not always imply dissociation; there are always numerous intersecting causes of a therapist's fluctuations in consciousness. And although many psychoanalysts see the primary cause of the therapist's countertransference reaction as reflecting the patient's use of dissociation; as stated above, it is also possible and likely that the therapist's own vulnerability to dissociative processes within herself influences the patient's dissociative process. Dalenberg (2000), in a study of patients' reactions to clinicians' countertransferences, found that patients are well aware of their therapists' emotional responses to them and find it disturbing when they deny or mask their reactions.

What I emphasize here is the importance of attending to the "here and now" moment-to-moment experience of attending to our *own* dissociative states. Therapists who work with trauma survivors and patients with dissociative experiences will inevitably find themselves dissociating—unable to think, contain, and symbolize the patient as a subject. The affective immediacy of the clinical moment is easily lost. Restoring it requires a close monitoring of our own internal dissociative states. We need to be aware of the pressure to dissociate and, in spite of it, to do our best in the struggle to symbolize and maintain an intersubjective awareness of the patient and their bodies as well (Newirth, 2016).

## Micro-level dissociation in the analyst as an "early warning system" defense

Working with trauma patients, I have noticed a specific type of acute dissociative countertransference response. Sometimes, a moment of acute dissociation has occurred within me *at the moment just prior to their disclosing unbearable traumatic material.* This happened with Helen in multiple instances; for example, just before she began relating explicit details of her childhood experience of sexual abuse, I became distracted, vaguely disinterested, and confused. This occurred again when she began to have the courage to describe the visceral sensations of her abuse; right before she went into the details, I lost my concentration and momentarily could not remember what we were talking about and why. It was as if I was involuntarily forcing myself away from what she was saying to avoid knowing the truth of what she endured. In my own experience, disclosures involving children, specifically our patients as children being raped or tortured, may cause this countertransference response right before the disclosure fully takes place.

Bromberg (2003) writes that dissociation can act as an "early warning system," anticipating potential affect dysregulation before it arrives. This sudden affective hyperarousal touches an area of unprocessed developmental trauma and which is mentally unbearable and thus unavailable to cognition. We turn away before the full "tsunami" of the trauma hits us (Bromberg, 2008). If not recognized, this "early warning system" can lead to more chronic and subtle forms of countertransference dissociation intended to protect us from vicarious traumatization, which can lead to a vicious cycle of dissociation in our patients as well.

## Embodied empathy and projective identification

The vital and disturbing relationship between empathy and vicarious traumatization is worth examining more closely. As emphasized above, psychotherapy and psychoanalysis are not intellectual pursuits; they require a "psychosomatic" immersion in another human being's primitive mental experiences. Patients in the grip of primitive mental states like Helen unconsciously search for another mind to help them face what is unthinkable and unknowable (Bion, 1962b; Eshel, 2019). This requires an authentic and emotionally resonant relationship—we need to be affected by our patients, and to do so means to absorb their feelings in ways that are often disturbing and painful.

This type of "embodied empathy" (Sletvold, 2014), also referred to as "affective empathy" (Pearlman & Saakvitne, 1995; Shamay-Tsoory, 2011), is essential to fostering a healing relationship in which one knows the patient "from the inside out" (Bromberg, 1991). By doing so, we allow our patients to experience and use our mind as a source of containment and a safe base from which to explore and know what before was traumatic and unknowable (Cooper, 2016; Eshel, 2019).

Our very capacity to do this, however, is what also creates traumatic responses in us. Ghislaine Boulanger (2018) addresses this dilemma in "When is Vicarious Trauma a Necessary Therapeutic Tool?"

She emphasizes trauma's contagious quality and the painful yet vital relationship between vicarious trauma and dissociation, arguing that in long-term clinical engagements with survivors of massive psychic trauma, vicarious traumatization is a key part of helping patients process the traumatic material. Countertransference dissociation may protect us from vicarious traumatization, but at a cost.

We often do not recognize the ways we defensively dissociate from allowing patients "worming" their "way into the analyst's brain" (Rosenfeld, 1971, quoted in Schore, 2003, p. 84). Before Helen confronted me with my being "checked out," I was not conscious of my inability to resonate with what she was implicitly communicating. Reflecting on our sessions together, I was not very disturbed or alarmed by what was happening between us, despite the worsening of her nausea and gastritis and her increasing hopelessness and despair. On an affective level, I was not taking in what her body was communicating. In my own body, there was also a lack of sensation and feeling, an important indicator of unresponsiveness to a patient. Commenting on a patient similar to Helen, Aisha Abbasi (2014) writes:

> I had thought it was because of my great capability to not take things personally. I now realized that it was because I had been what might be best described as the opposite of the "James Bond martini style" of analyst: shaken, not stirred. I had felt stirred, intrigued … but, defensively had *not* allowed myself to be shaken to the core, to be sufficiently disturbed by him. Yet this is a prerequisite for every truly useful analytic process. (p. 120)

Similarly, Hans Loewald (1986) notes:

> Less spectacular, but more insidious and often more damaging, are behaviors of the analyst that are the results of inner defense against his countertransference reactions, such as rigid silences, unbending attitudes, repression or isolation of troublesome impulses, fantasies, or memories … the analyst … in his effort to stay sane and rational is often apt to repress the very transference–countertransference resonances and responses induced by the patient that would give him the deepest but also

the most unsettling understanding of himself and the patient. (quoted in Schore, 2003, p. 89)

Schore (2003) notes that we should replace the word "repress" with "dissociate" in this passage, as it better captures the experience of disruption in the continuity of experience, whose function is to ward off the unbearable.

Contemporary Kleinian and Bionian analysts refer to this process as being able to receive and contain projective identifications. Projective identification is an emotional form of communication, a way of processing and regulating primitive mental states and trauma by inducing these experiences in others. This process is akin to how a mother contains and metabolizes painful mental states in an infant. Projective identification is bidirectional, and in a mutually reciprocal process, the patient can take on our disavowed mental states, especially if we are dissociated from them.

These dissociated and chaotic bodily and affective states inevitably touch on the analyst's own anxieties and traumas, tempting us to hide from the torment. Because we are prone to "falling ill" with our patients (Borgogno, 2014), there is always a potential to assume a masochistic or sadistic stance as opposed to recovering in order to contain and help our patients bear and represent their experience (Diamond, 2020). Some psychoanalytic writing verges on idealization of the containing process without acknowledgment of how painful and difficult this is for the therapist, who is human and can only bear so much. This tendency mirrors the implicit idealization in our literature of the mother's ability to contain and metabolize the infant's mental states, without taking into account the subjectivity and limitations of the mother who is doing the caregiving. Idealized images of a "perfect containing mother/perfect containing therapist," absorbing any projection or emotional communication, courts masochism, vicarious trauma, shame, and defensive narcissism in the therapist. We all have limits.

## Dissociated enactments

My inability to contain Helen's projections and stay attuned to her suffering did not occur only in acute moments. There was also a more pervasive "macro-level" dissociative process between us of which I only gradually became aware. Helen and I were both unconsciously locked into a way of being with one another that felt immovable and lifeless.

Donnel Stern (2004) describes enactments as the "interpersonalization of dissociation." He views the analytic field as an interlocking configuration of self-states contributed to by both patient and analyst. Each self-state is connected to a personified other, and these self–other states shift continuously. If a self–other state that is intolerable to either the analyst or patient threatens to disrupt the interpersonal field, a dissociated enactment may occur. This is a last-ditch defense to ward off the unendurable "not me" state that threatens to emerge. These "not me" states are dissociated from both analyst and patient; they cannot be assimilated and symbolized because of their catastrophic traumatic origin.

In patients with complex trauma histories there is often a conscious "known" self–other state that obscures more dissociated "not me" states. I have found the four patient-therapist configurations described by Davies and Frawley (1994) clinically helpful in recognizing these "not me" dissociated enactments, which are prototypes of self–other states: the uninvolved parent/neglected child, sadistic abuser/helpless angry victim, omnipotent rescuer/entitled child, and the seducer/seduced (Davies & Frawley, 1994; Karpman, 1968). In chronic forms of countertransference dissociation, patients often experience our countertransference dissociation in the transferential terms of an uninvolved, neglectful parent.

Helen experienced me as "not getting it," being "checked out," being more of a robot than a human being. I was the unresponsive parent and she was the neglected child. What was dissociated—the "not me" in the enactment—was *my* rage towards her for placing me in the crosshairs of her trauma. In this "not me" self-state, I was enraged at being "forced" to be with her in her traumatic experience, as I had felt forced in residency to be in the inpatient unit and bear witness to all of the trauma and aggression directed at me.

Maltsberger and Buie (1974) attribute mental states of inattention, boredom, stupor, and fatigue to unrecognized hatred in therapists, especially when they are frightened of sadistic impulses towards the patient. An unconsciously hateful therapist then subtly takes on the feared role of the sadistic abuser, and the patient becomes the helpless angry victim.

Pulling away feels safer to the therapist, but in this false safety there is an emotional deprivation that the patient experiences and reacts to. The more Helen angrily responded to my pulling away, the more I felt the need to dissociate from my rage at her recriminations (see other examples of this phenomenon in Dalenberg, 2000). This type of "cold" dissociative anger led to a distancing between us and a disruption of my ability to fully experience the severity of her suffering and register it on a visceral psychosomatic level. This created a chronic deadened experience between us, self-sustaining in its chronicity (Chefetz, 2009). Although I often knew something was not working in my relatedness with Helen, I had a difficult time moving out of my dissociated stance.

## "Coasting" in chronic forms of dissociation

While Helen was recounting the minutia of her day, I found myself validating what she was saying, tacitly "going along" with Helen's words. Consciously, I thought I was facilitating a validating, non-obtrusive holding environment that would enable Helen to speak freely. What she was attuned to, however, was the emptiness in my words and my lack of authentic presence with her. Allan Schore (2009) describes numbing, avoidance, restricted affect, and *compliance* as essential aspects of the dissociative experience. On reflection, my "going along" with Helen was a form of a compulsive and dissociated compliance, giving a "glazed over" quality to the rapport and agreeableness that defended against fears of being attacked and exposed to Helen's raw emotionality.

This dissociated compliant attitude in the countertransference is similar in some respects to Hirsch's (2008) concept of "coasting." Hirsch reminds us of the difficulty in suspending attention to one's self-interest and listening carefully to others "all day long." He notes the danger of an analyst's failing to acknowledge the desire for personal comfort and equilibrium, and then colluding with patients to stay comfortable or maintain an equilibrium. "Coasting in the countertransference" reduces anxiety and cocreates a comfortable enactment, indulging compliance and passivity in both patient and analyst. I would add that coasting can happen not only out of dynamics of self-interest, but also for self-protection. A chronic dissociative countertransference can avoid unbearable affects, fantasies, and traumatic memories, leading to the analyst's failure to grasp the pulse of the clinical moment and get to what is potentially destabilizing for the patient and therapist alike.

## Dissociation as an evasion of authenticity

With Helen, this dissociated avoidance was complicated by disavowed aspects of my experience that led me to "hold myself together" in a deceptively "normal" way, a false coherence that hid excruciating truths about my own childhood trauma and pain. Despite our sessions seemingly going "smoothly," there was a lack of authenticity between us and within me, a kind of blandness leaning towards formality and conformity in my way of being. Traumatologists refer to this type of functioning as "the apparently normal personality" (ANP) (Van der Hart et al., 2006). This apparent normality enables one to dissociatively avoid unbearable mental states, creating a phobic response to the emotional parts of the personality (EPs), which then threaten to erupt in the form of agitation and somatic states. The ANP is thus chronically depersonalized and emotionally bland, with low body awareness, and is often focused on routinized daily functioning. Survival and safety are the priority.

This description bears some similarity to Bollas's (1987) depiction of a "normotic" way of being, an excessively normal but deadened existence that avoids psychic pain and vulnerability. Goldberg (2020) refers to this as a peculiar type of "pseudo-relatedness" that is not mere superficiality; it is a complex form of living as a dissociated subject. Psychic survival is assured if one gives up one's agency, and one's particular, embodied way of being and adapts to the will of the other, ensuring safety and survival (Goldberg, 2020). I am suggesting here the problem of the "normotic" or "apparently normal therapist," who seems objectively neutral and reasonable but is defensively shut down against the excesses and passions of existence.

Being an "apparently normal therapist" with Helen diminished my recognition of her unspeakable trauma. As I became gradually aware of my own anguish and rage, I realized I had not fully come to grips with the devastation she had gone through—the violence and horror of her experience and the depth of her suffering. About such avoidance Bion (2005) says bluntly:

I don't want to appear to be criticizing or running down my colleagues, but I have recently become more and more convinced
that psychiatrists and psychoanalysts don't believe in mental suffering … fundamentally they never get to the point of feeling that
the person who comes to the consulting room is actually suffering … it is a very curious thing indeed for an analyst with many
years' experience to discover that his patient actually suffers pain.
(p. 48)

Without being able to take in Helen's emotional communications and
genuinely register her suffering, I was not able to fully *be with* her
trauma and her as an *individual human being separate from me, with
pain*. Warren Poland (2018), reflecting on his fifty-plus-year career as
a psychoanalyst, notes that the hardest thing to learn is also the most
obvious:

… that the patient is "somebody else," and that it is the analyst's
respectful recognition of the patient as having a self in its own
right, distinct and with its own values, regardless of those of the
analyst … It is crucial for a patient, for any person, to be seen,
acknowledged, and appreciated for that person's unique self.
Being seen and being gotten, without being acted on for the sake
of the other's purposes—that is vital and essential. (p. 6)

## Finding a way out of dissociation

Being with trauma is interwoven with dissociation for ourselves and our
patients. There is no prescriptive strategy out of this dilemma; it is an
inevitable process we must endure if we are committed to being with our
patients in a genuine way. Recommendations to therapists who struggle
with vicarious traumatization and dissociation often involve engaging in
some type of "self-care" or personal therapy. These are of course necessary but, perhaps because of my stubborn nature, I resist taking advice
like this at face value.

What feels most essential is that we do our best to stay in a place of
authenticity and respect with our patients and find ways of being and coping with our own pain and trauma—our supervisors, warm colleagues,

and authentic engagement with our own treatment is of course essential. Having an ironic and dark sense of humor can also keep us grounded, as long as we have a "relational home" for these bleak places. Struggling with the death of his wife Dede, distinguished psychoanalyst and philosopher Robert Stolorow (2007) writes:

> What has enabled me to remain resolutely devoted to this project rather than succumbing to various forms of dissociative numbing (although I have done this too)? [sic] For one thing, staying rooted in one's own genuine painful emotional experiences [also] … key family members and close friends have shown consistent acceptance and understanding of my painful states, thereby providing them with a *relational home* wherein I have been able to live in them, articulate them, and think about them, rather than evade them. (p. 46, italics added)

Cultivating a mindfulness approach in observing my own dissociative states in the flow of the moment with patients has been useful for me as well. This process allows the creation of a permeable boundary as we take in what is happening within our bodies and immerse ourselves in our patient's present lived experience. Our consumerist culture tends to brand mindfulness as a self-help strategy, a cheap slogan or a goal one must achieve. This characterization obscures the simplicity and elegant power of the original term. As Mark Epstein (2018) notes, mindfulness was first used as an English translation of the Pali word *sati*, found in ancient Buddhist texts in 1881 at the height of British colonialism. *Sati* can more simply be translated literally as "remembering" or "presence of mind." Right mindfulness implies remembering "to keep an eye on oneself as opposed to absentmindedness, the kind of forgetting that happens when one is lost in thought" (Epstein, 2018, p. 152).

David Wallin (2007) emphasizes mindfulness as one of two essential components of a therapeutic stance; the other is mentalization. Wallin notes that while mentalization involves depth, mindfulness involves the *breadth* of the therapist's experience, an acceptance and surrender to the conscious moment. Mindfulness, described as our attempts at nonjudgmental bare attention, orients us to our feeling states and bodily awareness from one moment to the next, rendering our experience less concrete and more elastic, "full-blooded," and experientially real: "There is a paradoxical 'lightness of being' and urgency that breaks through 'the trance of helplessness'" (p. 310).

Of course, mindfulness was developed as a "one person" technique, and psychotherapy involves an immersive and relational encounter with another human being who is suffering, a crucial intersubjective difference that makes the practice of surrender and acceptance infinitely more challenging. Striving to be open to receiving unbearable suffering from another will inevitably create moments of dissociation to challenge our ability to stay with our embodied selves. Here I view the therapist's ability to practice mindfulness as a way of creating a permeable space of our own; a type of porous psychic membrane to keep us partially contained with what our patients are experiencing and how we are being affected by it.

A mindful stance allows us the possibility to be more present with ourselves and being with our patients in a dissociative moment, widening our attention and allowing us to feel more alive and embedded in our experiences with patients in an internal space, loosening our attachment to rational or cognitive processes (Safran & Muran, 2000). We can then observe better our oscillations of consciousness and presence in the moment-to-moment flow of sessions and be open to a more genuine recognition of the suffering we need to feel and name (Bornstein, 2020). This can lead momentarily to a renewed "love of life," with the accompanying pain and vulnerability that we all face when we leave our safe but deadening places of hiding.

## CHAPTER 6

# Shame

*Shame is pride's cloak.*

—William Blake

To bring to life how shame can disrupt the analytic consulting room, consider this experience: On a Thursday afternoon I am listening to Jill, a mother of two with depression, recount the details of her recent and still painful divorce from her partner of ten years. Suddenly, I hear the door of my waiting room open and some rustling of someone putting their coat on the rack and sitting down. I feel a flash of heat and a jolt course through my body—*I forgot about Mark!* In my session with Mark on Tuesday, he asked to meet for an additional session, and I must have mistakenly put him in my schedule at the same time as Jill's session.

Mark, a thirty-six-year-old single schoolteacher struggling with chronic depression, was recently connecting online with a man he was interested in. During our session on Tuesday, Mark was able to put into words how frightened he was of his interest in this man, in part because it stirred his own desire, which made him feel like a "creep." Insecure and self-conscious about his shortcomings, Mark spent a good deal of time in our work together attacking himself for his passivity and feeling hopeless about his prospects for meeting someone. Over the past several weeks, however, he was slowly beginning to recognize that his relentless self-criticism and hopelessness were in part a protective shield against others' getting close to him, erected so that he could avoid feeling his erotic longings, this "creep" that lurked inside of him. At the end of our last session, he sheepishly asked for another appointment, and we talked about him feeling closer to me but feeling some sense of dread over what that means. Over the two years we had been working together, Mark had not asked for an additional appointment or so clearly articulated his anxiety over his desire. And now he's sitting for his appointment in my waiting room, but I am in a session with Jill. How could I have done something so damn incompetent and careless!

It is difficult to write this vignette and begin a chapter on writing about the experience of "countertransference shame," which is essentially (and shamefully) a chapter about my shame as an analyst. Saturated with images of excrement, weakness, and degradation, shame is hot blooded, full bodied, and disorientating. Shame is also complicated, embedded in a web of unbearable affects, psychic conflicts, fantasies, and trauma defying a simple definition (Wurmser, 2015). Experienced as a kind of toxic substance, it is reflexively avoided at all costs. Rooted in self-consciousness, shame is a fundamental part of our existence with others, and we feel shame when our self-presentation is threatened (Thomason, 2018). This heightened self-consciousness leads to the danger of acknowledging shame, which leads to feeling shame about shame. This process can quickly spiral into unbearable negative mental states of disintegration and self-loathing that lead to more hiding—the dreaded downhill "spiral of shame." Highly contagious as well, shame spreads quickly, wreaking havoc in the analytic setting where both the analyst and patient will be susceptible to its damaging effects from either person.

Shame lies uncomfortably close to the core of psychoanalysis, which is in a sense about uncovering what is hidden and unbearable, revealing what has been hitherto concealed. The essential psychoanalytic situation—two people without any preformed agenda, in an enclosed space, one privately sharing intimate details with the other—is a setup for an experience of shame. In almost every therapeutic session some overt expression or subtle manifestation of shame, humiliation, embarrassment, or disgrace is present (Morrison, 1989; Wurmser, 1977).

This is certainly the case for our patients due to the inherent asymmetry of disclosure in the relationship. Sharing intimate details with someone who is not reciprocating in the same way is a setup for shame regardless of the context. As one of my patients pointed out to me, "I have no idea whatsoever what you are really thinking or feeling, and I am putting myself out there for you to see it all and you can sit there nodding your head—and is this meant to help me?" Often patients feel exposed by our gaze alone, and despite our efforts not to shame them, we express ourselves inadvertently through our body language, tone of voice, and what we decide to focus on. We can easily convey criticism, ridicule, or aversion towards patients at their most vulnerable moments. Our patients are subject to our patronizing judgments, our failures of understanding, and our potential for being bored and disinterested in what they have to say.

What often goes unnoticed, however, are our own experiences of shame and how the analytic situation can provoke shame in us. We need to be able to "let the air in" (DeYoung, 2015) and face this unbearable emotion to feel less shame about our shame. Although our gut reaction may be to proceed with caution or avoid shame, it is also important to remember that shame should not be therapeutically bypassed (Danielian & Gianotti, 2012). Our daily experience of shame in the consulting room is rarely addressed head on. Ruth Stein notes that "There are no descriptions of how it feels for us analysts to really be proven wrong, of the subtle discomfort we feel when we sound off track, of the apprehension and anxiety in appearing ignorant or mistaken, and of having to grope occasionally for the right words, metaphors and intuitions, only to be corrected by the patient" (1997, p. 120).

Wherever there is intimacy and vulnerability, shame is lurking in the shadows, waiting to destroy relatedness and safety. In her wonderful chapter entitled "The Analyst's Sense of Shame," Adelman (2016) describes more than fourteen ways we experience shame in the consulting room, including failing to meet our patients' expectations, shame over our own fantasies about our patients, the shame of our own self-interest and power, and the shame of being the one to cause discomfort in our patients by asking them to tell us about traumatic events. The list is of course endless. Ladany and colleagues (2011) in their study on therapist shame identify several areas where therapists self-report shame, including making mistakes such as forgetting key details about a patient or falling asleep in a session, bodily function difficulties, and sexual behaviors by the patient. Therapists interviewed indicated that to various extents the therapeutic relationship was affected by their shame. Complicating this picture is that our shame is often hidden and can have unknown effects on our patients. As Mollon (2018) writes, "Shame that is overt and exposed is like a fox forcibly dug out of its lair, when the hounds have exhausted its capacity to flee and hide. Mostly shame lurks unseen" (p. xii). Our experience of shame as analysts is especially hidden, and perhaps like the fox that "lurks unseen," needs to be forcibly dug out. Rather than associating shame with weakness and withdrawal, we can instead face our vulnerabilities and cultivate the capacity for tenderness, compassion, and curiosity—allowing for a more nuanced experience and more empathic immersion with our patients (Danielian & Gianotti, 2012).

## Freud's shame

There are historical roots of neglect in addressing our experiences of shame. Freud, despite several important early contributions and insights about the nature of shame (for a detailed overview of Freud's contributions to shame see Morrison, 1989, pp. 22–29), clearly prioritized guilt over shame in his psychoanalytic theorizing. Freud's need to deny his own shame may have played a part in his neglectful and dismissive attitude—Freud viewed shame as feminine and primitive, aligned to visual and social aspects of the self. In contrast, guilt was associated with masculinity, autonomy, and individuality, not subject to penetration or vulnerability (Aron & Starr, 2013). Freud also appears to have struggled with his own shame of being seen through the hateful gaze of the ever-present anti-Semitism of his time. In a letter to his then fiancée Martha Bernays in 1883, Freud recounted a loud altercation between two Jewish families at a funeral he attended, writing, "We were all petrified with horror and shame in the presence of the Christians who were among us" (p. 65, quoted in Aron & Starr, 2013, pp. 52–53). Aron and Starr (2013) convincingly argue that through projected and displaced false dichotomies, Freud denied his shame to feel pride in his Jewish identity, emphasizing autonomy and masculinity over relatedness and femininity, which he relegated to categories of being immature and inferior.

Psychoanalysts continued this dismissal of shame for decades with some exceptions (Fenichel, 1945; Lynd, 1958; Nunberg, 1955; Piers, 1953) until the pioneering work of Helen Block Lewis. Lewis (1971) introduced shame as an essential aspect of psychoanalytic work, distinguishing it from guilt along phenomenological and developmental lines. She importantly highlighted how unidentified and unanalyzed shame is responsible for many treatment failures and therapeutic impasses. Her work inspired an eclectic group of psychoanalysts, self-proclaimed "shamenicks," who studied the nuances of shame in the therapeutic encounter and their often hidden and powerful effects on both the patient and analyst. Relational and intersubjective psychoanalytic perspectives shed light on the highly contagious and relational aspects of shame, where the analyst can be the initiator or maintainer of a shame state in the analytic process. If the analyst feels shame, a shame-prone patient can feel ashamed of sensing shame in the analyst, which can create a vicious cycle of shame that can lead to negative therapeutic reactions or therapeutic impasses (Aron & Starr, 2013; Broucek, 1991).

Shame is currently the central focus of numerous approaches outside of psychoanalysis as well, including trauma studies, cognitive psychology, and ethics. Healing from shame has gone "mainstream" with authors such as Brené Brown, whose TED talk on shame in 2012 currently has more than 14 million views (Brown, 2012). The astonishing popularity of discourses on shame speaks to the ubiquity of shame in our lives in the digital age, where anybody can easily access deeply personal information about anyone in an instant, leaving us in a perpetual state of anticipating being humiliated. Our contemporary internet-based social media culture is a shame-based culture, with some lamenting its deleterious effects on the shamed among us (Ronson, 2015) and others making the case for the importance of shame in social justice and political activism (Jacquet, 2015).

## Acute shame in the analyst

To describe the various ways our shame can affect the analytic process, it is useful to describe what happens in slow motion when we experience acute shame with our patients. Returning to my session with Jill, my experience of shame began with a vague and anxious apprehension of some movement in my waiting room. An anticipatory "shame anxiety" in the pit of my stomach erupted within me, a visceral sense that something was going to go wrong (Levin, 1967). As I suddenly realized my error, this ominous bodily feeling gave way to a surprising break in my ordinary conscious experience—my experience collapsed into one realization: "I forgot my session with Mark!" While guilt and shame were both operating here, the primary experience I felt in the moment was shame, perhaps because of the visceral and interpersonal shock of experiencing my mistake in the moment with Jill, who was alert to my facial expressions and my sudden awkward body posture.

In contrast to guilt, which is about what one has done wrong, shame is experienced as *being* wrong, defective, ugly, or damaged—the whole self is implicated (Herman, 2012). Although some authors label guilt, in contrast to shame, as a developmentally mature affective state (e.g., Tangney & Dearing, 2002), I regard guilt as distinct from shame (although one can feel both in succession, as in this example) and see each as having its own developmental trajectory with a spectrum of primitive to mature variations (cf. Aron & Starr, 2012; Carveth, 2006). There is also often a blurring between guilt, shame, and the subsequent fear of punishment which are experienced together in more primitive mental states (Wurmser, 2003).

Guilt and shame can also be sequentially tied together in reaction to angry feelings. One common clinical scenario involves an acute moment of shame, followed by a flash of anger and subsequent self punishment. This entire sequence can occur rapidly, lasting only seconds (Danielian & Gianotti, 2012; H. B. Lewis, 1971). Guilt about anger leads to self punishing thoughts which are experienced in the moment after shame, and anger is then directed back at the self. If this persists, resentment results from this shame-anger-guilt sequence, where anger is then directed back at the other, rather than back onto the self (Danielian & Gianotti, 2012). (See Chapter 3 on Dread for a more detailed examination of countertransference guilt.)

Returning to my experience with Jill, this full-blooded experience enveloped me, and I began to lose the thread of Jill's speech and became self-absorbed, castigating myself for my error. Lewis (1971) describes this shame reaction as a "wince, jolt or wordless shock." This state of shock is accompanied by a split in consciousness: a shamed "bad" self and the critical gaze of a shaming other with no other capacity for reflection or thought. Adam Philips notes that in acute shame "there must be no mental space for second or third thoughts about what has happened and is consequently happening. There is simply the torturer and the tortured. Shame is a figure for the mind colonized" (2019). In that shameful moment, there is a wish to void oneself entirely to escape this torture. The metaphors we use capture this wish for self-annihilation: We want to "sink through the floor," "crawl in a hole and die," "disappear forever," or "get off the planet."

Those of us who are "shame prone," because of our temperament interwoven with early childhood experiences of shame, are more susceptible to these moments of rupture. There is evidence that sensitivity to interpersonal events and a heightened self-awareness—traits many therapists possess—can render one more vulnerable to self-blaming and feelings of shame (Tangney & Dearing, 2002).

I can certainly relate to this, being a "shame prone" person myself. Growing up overweight with apraxia and learning disabilities left me vulnerable to being mocked and ridiculed, desperately searching for ways to hide or conceal myself to avoid humiliation. We often discuss these types of painful childhood experiences as a tool to increase our capacity for empathy for others who are suffering. While this is of course true to some degree, it is worth keeping in mind that experiencing shame often interferes with our empathic responsiveness. In my example above, in an instant, my empathic attunement with Jill vanished. Derailed by my own emotional experience, I became more self-focused and concrete, trying to manage my own shame (Tangney & Dearing, 2002). One irony among many about shame is that although it is experienced as essentially relational, with a preoccupation with being seen, its effects render one insular and self-involved.

## Bypassed shame in the analyst

As Mark sat in the waiting room, I struggled with my shameful choices. "How much can I disclose to Jill and Mark about my mistake? How can I talk with Mark about this, and how should I address this with Jill, who is clearly needing me to be present and attuned with her pain at this moment?" Reflexively and obsessively, I wanted to cover up my error and make excuses for my mistake. In retrospect, this was my effort to detoxify and rid myself of a shameful state of mind. Shame is often experienced as a brief moment of painful feeling followed by a lengthy episode of obsessive thought or speech (M. Lewis, 1992). Although overt in my case with Jill, this process can be quite subtle and can happen in an instant with only a brief register of the initial shame response. This is often referred to as bypassed or unfelt shame (Lansky, 2007; Lewis, 1992). In contrast to overt shame, which involves excessive feeling with little thought, bypassed shame involves excessive thought or speech but little feeling (Scheff, 1987). Consider the astonishing number of words we use to talk indirectly about shame: "ridiculous, foolish, silly, idiotic, stupid, dumb, disrespected, helpless, weak, inept, dependent, small, inferior, unworthy, worthless, trivial, shy, vulnerable, uncomfortable, embarrassed, thin skinned, self-conscious, sensitive, disconcerted, awkward, blushing, ignominious, improper, indecent, unchaste, demeaned, belittled, slandered, debased, defiled, disfigured, demoted, disgraced, dishonored, degraded, contemptible, mortified, scorned, worthless, and humiliated" (Herman, 2012; Steiner, 2015). These words provide a "cover" for shame, a way of both revealing and concealing what feels unbearable to look at directly. In subsequent sessions with Mark, it became clear that my unfelt shame and dread over our erotic excitement of a closeness between us was the culprit in my shameful error. (See Chapter 4 on Erotic Dread for more details about this.)

Also, despite shame having universally defined characteristic bodily and somatic expressions—including downcast eyes, blushing, submissive body postures, and hesitant speech—these physical expressions of shame quickly slip away and hide from view, leaving only traces: bodily agitation, self-effacing comments that expand into hilarious monologues, hesitation, mumbling, a flash of irritation, long pauses, rapid speech, or even a shame-provoking display that may appear shameless to defensively ward off being shamed; that is, being shameless as a reaction formation against shame (Tangney & Dearing, 2002; Wurmser, 2015).

Realizing my scheduling error and feeling shame in my session with Jill, I appeared uncomfortable for a moment and then began to smile and laugh nervously, with my tone of voice slightly increasing.

Jill picked up on my change in demeanor and became distracted, her eyes glazed downwards with a slightly hunched-over posture. She began to speak in an emotionally distanced manner. When we later talked about this experience after I apologized to her for my error, Jill still felt that *she* had done something wrong and was convinced that at that moment she was boring me. Jill, already prone to self-blame and shame, took my nonverbal signs of shame as confirmation of her own self-degradation.

## A necessary apology?

Because situations like this can cocreate and maintain shame-inducing spirals that can have a negative impact on treatment, it is important that therapists share responsibility with their patients in these cocreations (Dalenberg, 2000). This requires an apology and an acknowledgment of what has taken place on the part of the analyst. A sincere apology conveys an understanding of the patient's predicament and empathy for what he is going through. Usually, a failure to apologize indicates to a patient the analyst's need to save face and avoid shame at the patient's expense. As Lansky (2016) notes,

> Apology is an inevitable part of the process of repair that is absolutely vital to the attention to the health of the interpersonal bond and the vicissitudes of the injuries to that bond that are central and primary to the work of psychoanalysis and psychotherapy … when interruptions, large and small, occur in the analytic setting, some form of shame experience … is operative. (p. 134)

Of course, we can apologize too much, or in an insincere fashion, as a defensive way of warding off an attack by a patient. This process is expressed in some version of "It's my fault, everything you say is right, I am bad, I will do whatever it takes to make you happy so do not hurt me." These types of apologies are narcissistic maneuvers to eliminate our vulnerability to our patient's aggression and are of course not helpful but may occur spontaneously. In a shame-filled moment, I find myself torn between wanting to conceal and deny my error and to apologize profusely to avoid any kind of attack. A genuine apology stays in the discomfort of the moment and allows for some space to talk about what has happened.

## Envy and shame

An important source of shame in the consulting room is our envy towards our patients. Envy is a particularly difficult emotion to tolerate because it is a malignant and hateful attack on something valued and good that another person possesses, with a hateful wish to spoil and have total control over this goodness (Morrison, 1989). Our patients can be smarter than we are, more creative, more attractive, better parents, wealthier, more successful, and can have healthier relationships with their partners. They can also have a range of emotional experiences that we can only know of theoretically, having lived different and perhaps more interesting lives than we have.

Complex intersections of privilege and power within the therapeutic dyad create infinite possibilities for envy for both therapists and patients (Fors, 2018). So ubiquitous, it is difficult to imagine a treatment without the analyst experiencing some form of envy with a patient. Despite this, our envy towards our patients is rarely discussed, with notable exceptions (Allphin, 1982; Bodnar, 2004; Cooper, 2016; Fors, 2018; Hirsch, 2014; Safán-Gerard, 2019; Searles, 1979, 1986).

Envy and shame have a powerful mutually destructive relationship. If the object of our envy is idealized and powerful, our self is then viewed as weak, defective, inferior, failing by comparison. Destructive and hateful envious feelings towards our patients provoke shame in us, which can lead to defensively devaluing and pathologizing our patients to ward off our inferiority. Fors (2018), for example, observes that a highly successful person can be labeled as narcissistic or hypomanic based on our envy of their attributes and our feelings of shame over our comparatively limited successes.

Another hidden source of envy can be our patients' *successes* in their therapeutic work with us. Cooper (2016) refers to this as the analyst's envy of the patient's ability to receive help from us, playfully alluded to as "the analyst's envy of the patient's analyst." This can occur when we are able to give our patients what we were not able to receive in our own analysis; a result of our own failure to grieve and mourn the inevitable incompleteness of our own treatment. These envious feelings often involve fantasies about our patients being able to live more "freely" and "authentically" than we are (Cooper, 2016).

Feeling overtly envious towards our patients can also serve as a protection against a more unbearable and demeaning experience of shame. Morrison (1989) notes that shame is often missed in moments of envy because our attention shifts from experiencing a weak and shameful self-state to an exclusive focus on the envied and powerful object of our desire. Consciously experiencing envy then can be another means to lessen the pain of shame (Morrison, 1989). This occurred with my patient Kay, discussed in the chapter on racism. After she made a racist association, I consciously felt envy of Kay's white skin and privilege, but my shame over my own internalized racism and lack of privilege were not fully conscious. These moments of bypassed shame can lead to defensive anger and acting out on the part of the therapist, which usually takes the form of blaming or pathologizing the patient. Because shame and envy exist so closely together, overt envy can cover a deep-seated shame, which then can generate more envy.

## Greed and shame

"Greed is good," proclaimed Gordon Gekko, a sociopathic corporate raider in the classic 1987 film *Wall Street*. I doubt any psychotherapist or psychoanalyst would ever say this, at least out loud. As a profession of healers, we tend to eschew overt and mindless pursuits of wealth. We pride ourselves on our altruism, generosity, and steadfast commitment to helping others. Greed—an insatiable hunger for what we desire, often accompanied by impatience, inconsolability, ingratitude, and entitlement (Akhtar, 2015) is antithetical to values and ideals fundamental to our profession. We seldom talk about money and fees with our colleagues, and talking about fees and getting paid with our patients can feel riskier than talking about sex or violence (Berger & Newman, 2012). The reasons for this are of course complex. (For a good overview of these issues, see *Money Talks in Therapy* edited by Berger and Newman, 2012.) One important factor in our resistance to discussing these topics openly is our shame over our "greedy" desire for money and financial success.

Working through our shame around these topics and being more conscious of our greed can allow us to be more honest about our ethical conflicts and the choices we have regarding fees and billing policies. Having a conscious awareness of our greedy impulses can also be a helpful guide in potentially picking up and being receptive to unconscious enactments and projective identifications in our patients around their own conflicts involving greed (Abbasi, 2015). In my experience, feeling an urge to increase the fee for unclear reasons in reality, making mistakes on my billing, chronically undercharging patients, and not sending my statements on time to a patient can be indicators of a covered up shameful feeling of greed, and can signal some emergence of these themes in the therapeutic dyad.

## Wealth shame

Countertransference greed brings up intersections of power and privilege that can be an uncomfortable source of shame and guilt for us as well. Sadek (2020) employs the useful term "wealth shame" to describe the experience of an intense and castigating self-consciousness that haunts many of her patients. In an age of rapidly growing inequality, shame over our privilege and status can be both an ethical response to economic disparity (moral responsibility) and a manifestation of a more toxic pattern of shame which she describes as moral masochism. Wealth shame in this context can be a defense against pleasure, feelings of superiority, and a fear of being envied (Sadek, 2020). Our psychoanalytic community has historically had a conflicted relationship with our social class, money, and wealth, leading to a discomfort with openly disclosing our reactions to poverty, financial inequality, and class distinctions. Sadek (2020) notes that analysts who experience wealth shame but have not faced it, or who shy away from conversations about financial inequality may not recognize wealth shame in their patients as well.

## The still-faced patient

Another source of countertransference shame occurs when there is a sudden negative shift in our patient's feelings towards us. When a patient greets us warmly with a smile, we feel energized by their affection.

We are recognized and valued, bathed in the closeness of a fantasied merger with them (Mollon, 2018). We all love to be loved. This happens reflexively on a visceral level, often without our noticing the effects it has on us. These are the moments in therapy when we feel close and connected with our patients, sensing a mutuality and affection that carries us through difficult days. It stirs our unconscious fantasies of merger and our wishes to be loved universally and unconditionally.

Of course, the opposite holds true as well—if we experience a patient as cold or rejecting, and if we fail to elicit a smile or a laugh when we hope for one, we feel diminished and rejected. Our self-esteem falls, and in the absence of warmth or reciprocity we feel disconnected and deflated. While we often do our best to ignore or minimize these experiences, they have the potential to create a chronic background of shame that can affect our work as therapists.

This experience is reminiscent of the developmental model of shame proposed by Schore (Schore, 2003, 2019; Tronick, 2007). A child, newly acquiring a sense of self, anticipates an excited and attuned shared affective experience with a caregiver and instead unexpectedly experiences an affective misattunement—a disapproving look, an absent blank expression, or anger—triggering sudden stress and a shock-induced deflation in the child. Schore describes shame as the emotion that occurs in these moments of a rapid transition from an excited positive state to a deflated negative one. This core experience causes the child to feel as if they are falling apart without any safety or containment with the caregiver. In shame, one becomes a disintegrating self in relation to a dysregulating other (DeYoung, 2015).

When we meet our patients with warmth and caring and they are cold or disapproving, we are vulnerable to shame. Paying attention to our shifts in affective states and monitoring our own shame when our patients are rejecting towards us is especially crucial when a patient is emerging out of a false-self organization that prioritizes a need to please and comply with others. These patients are often compulsive "people pleasers" who need to satisfy the narcissistic demands of their caregivers. In crucial moments of authenticity there will be disappointment and frustration on both sides of the consulting room. This type of emotional turbulence is not nice or polite, and that is the point. When there is an emergence out of a regressive wish for total attunement, the therapist and patient will both make contact with shame (Mollon, 2018). It is the authentic self that is subject to shame, and likely to elicit disapproval or non-recognition by us. Our patients are under no obligation to love us or fulfill our narcissistic needs but, being human, we will react to this on some level.

## Case example

Julie, a recently married thirty-four-year-old woman with a history of depression, began a session telling me she was pregnant. Julie grew up in a home with an often-absent mother who struggled with psychosis and a father who was available but only on his terms. Over the six years of her analytic treatment, she struggled with her desperate longing for intimacy and to be known, conflicting with a wish to be obliterated and dead with no feeling or desire. Gradually she began dating and got married with a tenuous sense of hope about the possibility of a future.

Needless to say, Julie's disclosing her pregnancy was a poignant moment. I flashed a warm smile and spontaneously said, "Congratulations! Wow!" Julie, usually responsive and warm, looked down and with a tight smile said, "Thank you," with little affect. I was taken by surprise and felt deflated and suddenly ashamed by her muted reaction to my enthusiastic response. "This is going to be the end of me," she snapped. "This is what you wanted, I'm sure, but this is not what I want. I've got no place to hide anymore." After saying this, Julie became silent. I felt an irritated urge to remind her that this is what she wanted as well, and that I was on the side of her wanting to live, which is what she also wanted. These thoughts were a defense against my shame over her angry and unanticipated reaction. I did my best to stay with what she was feeling in the moment, and what emerged from Julie was a deep and until now unspoken anger at me for implicitly taking the side of her living when death was an escape and a freedom that she felt she needed to have in order not to feel trapped or beholden to others, including me.

What followed was a difficult period in our work together. We gradually and painfully began to talk about how she often "fed" me affection the way she had had to feed her mother in order to feel safe and to avoid shame at the possibility of me withdrawing or being angry with her. This came at the expense of her being able to feel and speak honestly about her disappointment in me and her wish for having a single life with no burdens of family life or having to raise children.

## Shame and our wish to heal all

Choosing to devote one's life to being with the emotional pain of others is an unusual career choice, and most of us decide to do this line of work because of deeply personal reasons that are not fully known to us at the beginning stages of our career. In my experience, both personally and working with clinicians, there is often an unconscious fantasy of healing an emotionally disturbed person we loved and needed from our childhood that hurt us. In childhood, we were helpless and vulnerable to this person's suffering and their effects on us. As clinicians, we do our best to help our patients in ways we could not in our past, with a hope that this will heal us from the psychic wounds that remain. There are numerous examples of this in autobiographical accounts of psychoanalysts, often involving a depressed caregiver and a sensitive child who was desperate and powerless to help. A notable example of this is D. W. Winnicott's fraught relationship with his depressed mother, as described in Kahr's 1996 biography.

This wish to heal our ghosts from the past, displaced onto our patients, can lead us to enact unconscious omnipotent fantasies of healing with them. Our fantasies of cure often also implicitly reflect a fantasy of an ideal patient who we anticipate will respond to our work with them (Cooper, 2016). When our grandiose aspirations fall short of this ideal, we are vulnerable to feeling shame and a defensive need to restore our sense of self-esteem by denial, anger, or some form of blaming the patient.

This is especially the case with our therapeutic failures. It is striking how we mark our treatments as successes to our colleagues, conveniently leaving out the people we were unable to help. Most narratives and case examples written and presented have a "happy ending" narrative—the patient presents with symptoms and conflicts, there are a series of enactments and impasses, and eventually the analyst and patient find a way forward and the patient improves. Lear (2003) states this well:

> The generic analytic case history that one reads in a journal has this broad structure: the analyst spends some time in confusion, there are false starts and stops, there is an impasse or two, suddenly the analyst finds the impasse is broken and can see an interpretive dynamic reason why and then there is great progress. Is this really the way analytic stories unfold? Or has an analyst's own wishes helped shape the story? And if an attuned analysand wants to gratify his analyst by presenting such a story, how many analysts are going to interpret that wish? (p. 7)

I must admit, reviewing the chapters of this book, that I also indulge in this shame-free narrative of patient success. We all know psychoanalytic work is messy, complicated, and incomplete. Our stumbles and missteps as clinicians are often shameful secrets we share only with trusted supervisors or our own analyst, and even in those protected spaces we do not always speak truthfully.

Patients who do not benefit from our work with them often do not have a voice in our literature or in our supervision and consultation with others. Facing up to these often hidden and silenced truths from patients would be painful but instructive for all of us. In order to be in our line of work, a cultivation and appreciation of limits, disappointment, and endings is vital. Cooper refers to this as a "slender sadness," an appreciation of the pathos of life (2016, p. 87). Quoting Beckett (1984), we try to "fail better" (p. 11) and bear our shame of failure. This is of course not an end in itself, but an ongoing process of living in the uncertainty of our ability to help our patients and being open to the possibility of our limitations.

Psychoanalysis often also isolates itself from other disciplines and clinical approaches because of this shame over our limitations. Much has been written in favor of widening the scope of psychoanalysis, the clinical efficacy of psychoanalysis and psychodynamic therapy compared with other treatments, and the importance of long-term psychodynamic treatments over short-term therapies (Shedler, 2010; Solms, 2018). While this is quite persuasive and true to a large extent, we often do not acknowledge the limitations of what we can provide as psychoanalysts and the demonstrated efficacy of other treatments available to patients that could be helpful to them.

It is revealing that in my experience, most psychodynamically trained clinicians will be comfortable referring a patient for a medication evaluation if they feel they need additional help with their symptoms but are less willing to refer them to a clinician for another psychotherapeutic approach—despite numerous studies demonstrating benefits from other non-psychodynamic psychotherapies (Wampold & Imel, 2015). (There are of course exceptions to this lack of acknowledgment of other therapies, including Garrett, 2019; Howell, 2020; McWilliams, 2004; Summers & Barber, 2010; Wachtel, 2007.) This may be due to an unspoken and perhaps unfelt shame on the part of the analyst, who cannot bear not being able to heal the patient herself, and her shameful jealousy over other treatments that may work more effectively (see Chapter 8 on Jealousy).

## Case example

Avni, a twenty-eight-year-old married physician, began treatment with me for persistent and debilitating anxiety about the health of her newborn son. She found herself unable to stop checking her son's body for signs of a genetic disorder she was convinced would end his life or cause permanent brain damage. Despite numerous consultations with physicians at several prominent teaching hospitals who reassured Avni that her son had no such issue, she continued to engage in compulsive checking behaviors and felt tortured by intrusive thoughts of her son's possible catastrophic diagnoses.

Avni began twice-weekly appointments with me but continued to worsen despite my best efforts to help her. When I recommended that she increase the frequency of her sessions or consider a medication to help with her debilitating obsessions, she strongly disagreed because of her concerns about her breastfeeding while using the medication and feeling she could not spend any more time away from her baby. I felt frustrated and upset about her resistance to more treatment and her lack of progress. After a consultation with a trusted supervisor, I realized that my frustration was in part due to an omnipotent fantasy of being her rescuer. I had not considered other treatment options for her out of my shame in not being able to help her and live up to my grandiose expectations of being the person to heal her. With help from a colleague, I was able to refer her to a therapist who special-ized in obsessive-compulsive disorder. Avni began intensive but brief exposure response prevention therapy (ERP) with significant improve-ments over the course of one month and was grateful to her ERP thera-pist for years afterward.

## Suicide and the shadow of shame

Our omnipotent ideals of healing are completely demolished when a patient commits suicide. The devastation we feel in the face of this tragedy is profound and difficult to put into words. Hearing about the suicide of her patient, Nina Coltart describes her reaction being

> … profoundly shocked. It was as if the event was a complete bolt from the blue. It was quite an odd phenomenon; I was made newly aware of the kind of splits, conscious and unconscious, engineered and hidden, that we have to live with in our attitude towards our work. (1993 p. 54)

I would add that we also feel torn to shreds with shame, feeling that something within us is falling apart.

This terrible shame interrupts our ability to feel and work through our grief and loss. We are forced to face up to the painful realization of our helplessness in being a healer to everyone. Our narcissistic fantasies of healing usually serve in traumatic situations as a protection against helplessness, but of course in a completed suicide we are faced with the extreme limitations of our ability to help others. It is the "ultimate narcis-sistic injury" to a therapist's ideal of being a healer (Gabbard, 2014, p. 247).

In her insightful and revealing qualitative research on the impact of suicide on clinicians, Jane Tillman (2006) describes the shameful shat-tering of our ideals and the subsequent paranoid persecutory projec-tions that follow. In the aftermath of a completed suicide attempt by her patient, Dr. A, a participant in the study, describes the initial shock to her professional ideal, stating, "I really thought if you were good enough you could help almost everybody. That these things only happen to clinicians who miss something, and I learned that this is not true … This was a turning point, a reorienting point" (Tillman, 2006, p. 164).

After this shock, Dr. A struggled with persecutory projections of shame and condemnation from others:

> [Dr. A] went to a memorial service at the hospital for the patient and that she felt one particular colleague actively blamed her for the patient's death. She thought several people engaged her in a manner that communicated "you fucked up," … Dr. A noted that she was already in an isolated position as a psychoanalytic clinician in a psychobiological, cognitive/behaviorally oriented training program. This intensified her feelings of self-scrutiny, and her fears that her colleagues would use the suicide of her patient to point out how ineffective or dangerous psychodynamic treatment is to seriously disturbed patients … on several occasions Dr. A felt they were saying, "Why should we listen to you, look what happened to your patient." (Tillman, 2006, p. 165)

Fortunately, with a supportive supervisor and analyst, Dr. A was able to work through her shame and engage in the transformative work of grieving and mourning for her patient and her ego ideal as a psychotherapist:

> Dr. A felt a greater sense of paradox around helpfulness and helplessness, and around feeling both more responsible and less responsible for her patients. She talked about a greater sense of her fallibility and there being a certain comfort in that. Finally, Dr. A noted that she seemed "to take things in even more deeply than I did before," observing that this extended to her role as a clinician and also to her personal life. (Tillman, 2006 p. 166)

Having lost several patients to suicide, I can personally relate to Dr. A and the lasting effects of this shame as well as the difficult but crucial need for grieving. Long after the events took place, my grief was often laced with a persecutory anxiety of feeling like a failure in the eyes of the world, including my most trusted friends and colleagues. This felt endless, because the more shame I felt, the more I compulsively relied on fantasies and perceptions of how I was being seen. This reaction then exacerbated my vulnerability to shame and increased my paranoid and persecutory defenses by attributing power to others that they do not have (Kilborne, 2002; Lansky, 2005). This anticipatory shame, transformed into a paranoid type of shame, shielded me from a deeper, more profound helplessness that I needed to face in order to grieve and honor these patients I cared for.

## The value of shame

This chapter has primarily focused on how shame, both experienced and bypassed, can negatively affect our analytic work and relatedness with patients. It would be worthwhile to note that I am not advocating for a shame-free existence. There are primitive and toxic forms of shame that cause psychic disintegration and phobic withdrawals from reality— these experiences of shame cause suffering and require a compassionate space for healing and working through. There are other, less toxic forms of shame that allow us to function in society as responsible adults. The capacity to feel shame serves an important social function, maintaining social standards of mutuality and respect (Danielian & Gianotti, 2012). Following Aristotle, Wursmer (2015) describes the Greek definition of a variant of shame, "*aidos*," for the protective attitude of shame, a character trait of avoiding self-exposure or disgraceful acts with reverence and a sense of honor and integrity of one's self-image.

Acting shamelessly with our patients without modesty or restraint can lead to arrogance and acting out in the consulting room (see Chapter 1 on Arrogance and for a comprehensive discussion on shamelessness, see Akhtar, 2018c). Shame can be conceptualized as a prosocial affect (Sedgwick & Frank, 1995), which involves moral responsibility. When we treat our patients or colleagues with disregard or with disrespect, along with guilt there will be some form of shame that needs to be faced and accepted.

CHAPTER 7

# Hopelessness

*Sometimes hope for the right thing can be reached only through an immersion of prolonged and harrowing hopelessness.*
—Stephen Mitchell, *Hope and Dread in Psychoanalysis*

Since childhood, the Greek myth of Pandora fascinated me. Giving in to her curiosity, Pandora opens a forbidden vessel (often translated as a "box") that unleashes all of the misery in the world, including vanity, slander, envy, and sickness. Left behind in the vessel is *hope*, which apparently was there all along with the suffering now brought upon the earth. The myth never explains why hope is in the vessel in the first place and why it stays inside. This always left me unsettled and a bit confused—is hope the only good left by the gods for humanity to discover to withstand all of the misery in the world? Or is hope at the bottom of all of the evil and misery we suffer with, hidden from view but waiting to wreck us?

While the idea of hope is ambiguous in the myth of Pandora, psychoanalysts are ambivalent and sometimes downright skeptical about hope in our work with patients. There seem to be two conflicting perspectives on hope, both of which are in tension with one another

(S. Mitchell, 1993; Slochower, 2006). Some psychoanalysts see hope as a fixed regressive fantasy, creating a gap between the ideal and the actual, closing down the spark of desire in real life by fixating on an ideal future that can never be achieved. It is only by letting go and mourning this hopeful ideal that genuine desire and satisfaction become a possibility in reality (Boris, 1976). Others view hope, including "infantile" fantasies and yearnings, as essential to the process of transformation and psychic growth. These archaic and secret hopes do not need to be relinquished; they should instead be creatively brought back to life by the analyst so they can develop and grow though an authentic engagement with another (Balint, 1968; Winnicott, 1965).

Contemporary psychoanalysts have come to appreciate the ability to live in this tension of what hope can offer and hinder for our patients as well as ourselves. Hope is a complicated mix of wishes and needs, imagined solutions to early pain, trauma, and frustration, often embedded in fantasies of restoration, magical transformation, and retribution (Mitchell, 1993). Mitchell notes that the patient and analyst often "hope for the wrong thing" in the early stages of treatment, and it takes courage on the part of both to strive for an authentic hope that can be achieved: "By finding again and redefining his own sense of realistic hope, the analyst is able to find a voice in which to speak to the patient that is different from the voices of the patient's past" (1993 p. 214). This means at times sustaining some apprehension of hope in the face of a "prolonged and harrowing" hopelessness within the analyst, which is the focus of this chapter.

## Hopelessness in the analyst

Our experience of hopelessness is a familiar visitor to the analytic encounter, an unwelcome intrusion interrupting our faith in our ability to help our patients. Freud's (1937c) remark referring to psychoanalysis as an "impossible profession" (p. 248) is now a cultural cliché and defensively takes the sting out of this unbearable experience that we all fear and loathe in our clinical work. Jokes and clichés aside, however, the day-to-day struggles of being in the trenches with our experiences of hopelessness in our encounters with our patients remain largely unspoken.

Hopelessness is a difficult and exhausting experience to endure—it has a certain cognitive certainty in the way it feels which can undermine the inherent vitality and exploration in the analytic space. A peculiar deadening feeling emerges which grips our body and mind. The experience of a sinking sensation in one's abdomen or tightness in the pit of one's stomach is common, sometimes accompanied by feeling slightly dizzy or faint. One feels defeated by a conviction of there being no chance for growth or change.

In contrast to an open and vibrant atmosphere filled with vitality and play, or an angry arena where battle lines are sharply drawn, the experience of hopelessness is characterized by a sense of rigidity and deadness. Time feels warped and at a standstill; there is an agonizing sense of paralysis of movement and flow, which often leaves us feeling trapped and helpless. Human bonds with the patient collapse and we feel absorbed in our own endless rumination of there being no possibility of intimacy or relationality. Distressing negative thoughts attack our ability to focus and be present, such as "this treatment is going nowhere," or "this is a failure." An atmosphere of doom inhabits the analytic space and often leads to feelings of anxiety, inadequacy, and shame.

Under less oppressive circumstances there is a dynamic interplay between the patient and the analyst with each party emotionally affecting the other. In order for the analytic space to be a place of growth and transformation, the analyst strives to navigate between her experiences of doubt, uncertainty, and confusion to arrive at an understanding of what is happening and in the process help the patient have an in depth experience of his psychic life.

Contemporary analytic theory positions our countertransference as an unavoidable and indispensable tool we use in the service of furthering the analytic process. Over the course of psychoanalytic theorizing, however, three perspectives on countertransference have been noticeable, as described by Oelsner (2013). Freud originally intended to define our countertransference as an obstacle to the analytic process, based on one's own personal history and biases that interfere with free floating attention and unconscious communication between the patient and the analyst (Freud, 1910d). Later Kleinian and object relations theorists viewed countertransference as a possible consequence of projective identification of the patient's self or internalized objects (Heimann, 1950; Racker, 1957) and therefore a helpful source for understanding the patient's internal world. Following Bion, many contemporary analysts now view countertransference as central to a reverie-based method of emotional containment for the patient's unbearable affects and fantasies (Bion, 1963; L. Brown, 2019).

In the emotional storm created in the analytic space between our patients and ourselves, our ability to contain and hold unbearable mental states, including hopelessness, becomes fundamental to our analytic task: the promotion of psychic development and growth for the patient. We do our best to invite into our mind the experiences of conviction and doubt, certainty and confusion, and vitality and deadness to allow for the relational analytic process to take hold. We retain optimism and safeguard our vision of a patient who is less in the grip of suffering. Similar to an artist who "sees" the shape and image of what she is about to create, analysts also envision what patients would be like with the lessening of the burden of neurotic misery (Loewald, 1960).

The collapse of this very analytic vision constitutes the essence of hopelessness. When hopelessness invades the analytic space, what before was seen as possibility and success in imagining a future collapses. In an often rigid and concrete fashion, it feels as if there is no vision or potential for growth. Our analytic vision stumbles and we are left with a pervasive sense of stupor and dead ends with no possibility of creation. This can occur with varying levels of severity and conviction; even the degree of awareness of one's hopelessness can vary.

For the sake of conceptual clarity, it may be useful to separate "acute" experiences of hopelessness that occur unexpectedly and then recede out of consciousness from "chronic" forms of hopelessness experienced in situations described as impasses, stalemates, or "negative therapeutic reactions" (Freud, 1923b). These difficult situations lead to profound struggles and inevitable enactments that can place a heavy burden on the analytic space and disrupt the analyst's equilibrium. This often leads to defensive reactions on the part of the analyst's belief she can be helpful, have some understanding of what is happening, or envision a future for the patient.

## Acute hopelessness

During the moment-to-moment progress of an analytic session, the analyst receives and experiences a flow of associative material, emotional reactions, and wishful impulses which are potentially useful guides in aiding the analytic process. Often, we are gripped with an emotion or a stream of thought, which on the surface does not have a direct counterpoint in the patient's associative material. However, being responsive to such reactions and observing them carefully can lead to a deeper emotional understanding of a patient's internal conflicts and internalized objects, especially when there is an intensity to our reactions that does not correspond to the clinical situation (Racker, 1957).

An important note of caution is warranted, however. Our emotional response to patients is *our* own unique subjective experience, which can relate to our patients' associations and behaviors in the relational coconstructed space that led to that reaction. The simple truth is that we never fully know why we feel what we do—remaining open and curious about our reactions without grasping for ready-made or facile explanations for our experience is crucial. As Renik (2006) notes: "An analyst's perceptions are constantly influenced by a variety of conscious and unconscious idiosyncratic factors, and the analyst can never know, in any given moment, to what degree or entirely in what manner his or her listening is being shaped by highly personal thoughts and feelings of which he or she is unaware" (p. 88).

Concrete explanations for countertransference reactions such as "he put his anger inside of me and made me feel angry" can be helpful when the analyst has been flooded by her emotional reactions to her patient and requires a method of creating an observing space to restore analytic balance and treatment, but these explanations can also be used defensively to avoid more personal and painful fantasies the analyst suffers when difficult situations unconsciously begin to affect her narcissistic balance. The analyst might then be tempted to believe that her subjective conscious reaction is concretely related to the patient's direct experience. Fink (2007), highlighting this danger, writes:

> The underlying assumption—that the analyst knows herself so well that she knows what part of her reaction to the analysand is subjective and what part of it is objective—is fundamentally flawed; for the analyst continues not to know all of her own motives even after a very lengthy analysis—such is the nature of the unconscious. (p. 187)

Falling into concrete explanations of one's countertransference reactions often comes in the form of an empathic rupture with the patient when the analyst is listening to something new or unexpected which can make her lose her bearings, or when her formulation of a moment in treatment no longer applies to what she is listening to in the session (Faimberg, 2001, 2013; Fink, 2007). Turning to theory-based countertransference explanations can often be a defensive rationalization when the analyst is faced with doubt or the unknown (see Chapter 3 on Dread. As Schwaber (2005) notes, we strive in "listening to learn what we don't yet know, to linger with a nuance that might not fit our course, that might indeed reveal to us that we were not listening ... in this ... open ended effort" (p. 791).

With this caution in mind, however, acute experiences of hopelessness in the analyst can be valuable guides in uncovering previously unfelt conflicts and fantasies with our patients. Not taking our hopelessness at face value and being curious about what it may signify open up opportunities and the possibility of genuine hopefulness.

## Doubt

One aspect of acute hopelessness that can enter the analytic space is a profound and sometimes sudden sense of doubt in the analyst's mind—doubt about whether the treatment will work, or if the analyst is even "getting it," that is, understanding what the patient is trying to communicate. The sense of knowing, having insight or meaning is lost in this moment and a disturbing feeling of confusion invades the analyst's mind. This can occur if the patient's associations do not seem to follow any psychic logic and are vague and incoherent, or the patient's tone of voice and manner of speech convey hopelessness and defeat. Our ability to understand is often protected by a certain degree of idealization—when we are faced with the limits of our comprehension, our illusion of omniscience crumbles and we may experience a moment of hopelessness that can obscure our ability to stay emotionally with what the patient is unconsciously communicating (Mitchell, 1993).

In these moments, the analyst's reaction of doubt and confusion might convey an unconscious communication from the patient. Feldman (2009) writes persuasively about such communication of doubt in the moment-to-moment interactions in the analytic space in the analyst. He notes:

> In addition to the inevitable and appropriate doubts about his understanding and his work, the analyst is subjected to conscious and unconscious pressures from the patient, the aim of which seems to be to fill him with uncertainty, confusion and doubt … it is a means of communicating something important about the nature of the patient's state of mind, his internal objects and their relationships. It may be a way of drawing the analyst into sharing a disturbing state of mind … on the other hand, the patient may project his own uncertainty into the analyst's mind freeing himself to embrace a state of manic confidence … finally, the patient may be driven by hatred and envy to attack the analyst's state of mind and derive perverse gratification from this process. (p. 217)

The analyst's capacity to serve emotionally as a container for these unbearable experiences necessitates her to first fully experience them and then "recover" back to her reflective stance to continue the analytic work: "It is important to recognize the extent to which this process reflects elements of the patient's state of mind, and represents the patient's need to have this recognized and experienced by the analyst … the analyst's capacity to reflect, in due course, on this situation, may enable him to deepen his understanding of the patient" (Feldman, 2009, p. 230).

## Loss

The acute experience of hopelessness in the analyst can also serve as a signal for the possibility of unfelt loss and mourning on the part of the patient. In a process of "concordant identification" (Racker, 1957), the analyst might experience the patient's unfelt grief over an early loss, as well as possible defenses against this grief.

What I have found crucial here is for us to face our own struggle with our unbearable losses, with all of the longings, anger, and grief that we carry with us. These experiences are often felt and reexperienced through the lens of hopelessness that occurs in the intersubjective space between the analyst and patient. In these situations, experiences of hopelessness (both for ourselves and our patients) are often simultaneously a method of expressing grief as well as warding off the intense pain and helplessness of true mourning, which requires confronting not only the loss of what we desire and long for, but also the fantasied hopes and dreams that were connected with the longed-for object as well.

Negativity and hopelessness as concrete realities can also be clung to as sources of solace and control to avoid mourning: "Fascination with the negative preserves the exciting, the perverse, magically omnipotent illusion that one can control what is uncontrollable" (Coen, 2003, p. 534). Woven into the experience of hopelessness is both the expression of loss and anguish, as well as a method in which the analyst and patient both shield themselves from the helplessness and pain of the loss.

## Case example

Lamar, a twenty-four-year-old first generation Jamaican American PhD graduate student in art history, sought consultation for chronic symptoms of low energy, low motivation, and difficulty with concentration in the context of his engagement breaking off one year prior. After a two-year engagement to his girlfriend of over seven years, their relationship ended after Lamar learned of his fiancée's infidelity. Struggling to get through the day and finish his thesis, Lamar denied feeling sad about his loss, noting, "I was sad for a while, now I feel just numb to it."

At first, Lamar was excited to engage in the psychoanalytic process and often agreed enthusiastically with my interpretations and thoughts about what he was feeling. I was somewhat suspicious about his degree of agreeability but also hopeful and looked forward to seeing him. It seemed we were making progress and he was engaged and thoughtful about his associations and feelings.

A noticeable shift occurred, however, several months into the treatment after he began to struggle with procrastination over his written work. After several sessions of describing his struggles with writing his dissertation thesis in a dry, emotionally disconnected manner, I struggled to feel emotionally engaged with him and emotionally involved. His content lacked emotional depth; he appeared to be focused on his work, and wanted help with tips on breaking through his writer's block.

During one particular moment when he was again describing the details of what he needed to do to complete his thesis chapter, I suddenly felt a surge of hopelessness within me that lasted several minutes, which was in sharp contrast to my usual optimism in our relationship. It felt as though there was nothing left to feel, nothing to connect the two of us. In that moment, in a concrete way I felt that I had exhausted what I could do for him—he was lost to me emotionally and I felt like an observer, watching him from a distance, with no possibility of engaging or being with him. Was this hopeless reaction on my part a way of expressing my anger towards him for disrupting my feeling of needing to be helpful? This explanation felt somewhat true but did not resonate emotionally with me. I was already conscious of being frustrated with him, and this distinct feeling of acute hopelessness was of a greater magnitude and rendered me feeling we were emotionally far apart from one another.

Reflecting on this hopeless state, I remembered Lamar mentioned that before the breakup with his fiancée, they would sit and study together in their apartment on their bed, side by side, him introducing her to his favorite artists from Jamaica. This image brought up moments of loss from my own past similar to this, which left me sad and excluded, yearning for what was lost. I then remembered Lamar's dry, emotionally disconnected way of speaking about his thesis, and I felt hopeless again. These associations helped me realize that my hopelessness and our rather bland but cordial way of being together was a way of avoiding painful affects of loss, longing, exclusion, and helplessness that felt too unbearable for either of us to feel together.

These ideas helped me bear Lamar's defensive hopelessness better and stay closer to his lived experience. I began actively pointing out moments when he seemed to veer into intellectualized thoughts about his work or procrastination, which seemed to enliven our work together. Exploring Lamar's frozen grief and longing led to a deepening of the treatment and to further fantasies of lost hopes from his difficult childhood transitions to America without a consistent paternal figure, and their connection with the sudden loss of his lover.

This work with Lamar took another difficult turn after he ran into his ex-fiancée at an academic conference with another man. As we explored his grief, he felt a great deal of shock over seeing them together, but mostly he felt numb. After this episode, Lamar's hopeless thoughts flooded our sessions together and he began to doubt why he was in treatment, stating flatly, "Talking about this only makes me feel worse." Efforts to help him with these relentlessly negative thoughts by offering hope and support only furthered his pessimism and doubts about getting help. I slowly began to realize I was defensively warding off my own feelings of despair, frustration, and hopelessness by these offers of support, implicitly identifying with Lamar's unbearable loss.

I was frightened by his hopelessness because it led me to experience an unbearable deadened feeling in my body, buried losses I never allowed myself to feel or fully come to terms with. As I began to feel my own grief covered over by this deadened somatic hopelessness, I slowed down and let Lamar fully express his hopelessness in our work together. Lamar was hiding the full intensity of his disappointment, anger, and despair with me out of fear and sadness of what could happen between us if he did so. He implicitly believed I would abandon him or attack him if he expressed these feelings directly. This echoed what he experienced from his father, who had no patience for Lamar's more introspective and sensitive nature to others and often criticized him for being "soft." His initial agreeableness to my interpretations was not about the truth of their content; it had to do with Lamar eagerly wanting a connection with me and using these interpretations as a means of establishing a fusional conflict-free relatedness, defensively warding off any negative feelings about me that could interfere with this (Britton & Steiner, 1994).

With difficulty, Lamar began to give voice to his disappointment and hopelessness about my ability to help him. His vague generalized feelings of hopelessness gradually gave way to a more lived-in and immediate experience of despair and hopelessness in a specific relational context with me (Safran & Muran, 2000). This led to him being able to be more in touch with his pain and yearning for closeness and a wish for authentic contact. Allowing myself to be uncomfortably in touch with our losses, doubts, and hopeless feelings helped me tolerate Lamar's frozen grief and gave him the opportunity to have a more authentic voice in our work together.

## Chronic hopelessness

In contrast to acute moments of hopelessness, which the analyst can transiently experience and then recover from to aid with the analytic process, chronic experiences of hopelessness cause significant disruptions in the analytic work and can strain the analyst's capacity to remain engaged with the patient. The literature on impasses, negative therapeutic reactions, chronic narcissistic transferences, and "stuck" or "bogged down" analyses all speak to the difficult countertransference experiences the analyst endures in these circumstances. In these difficult moments, the analyst feels trapped in a one-dimensional space where there is no experience of growth or possibility of play—only hopelessness and dead space are permitted. Any positive movement or authentic intimacy is quickly dismissed and defended against by the patient or analyst. The message that seems to be omnipresent towards the analyst is "you mean nothing to me, this relationship is nothing."

Serious disruptions in the analyst's professional ego ideal (Giovacchini, 1993) can disrupt one's ability to maintain a therapeutic responsiveness to the patient, and reactive countertransference reactions can become truly difficult to manage. The analyst strives to make some meaning of this misery and emptiness, only to find herself confused and shut out. It is only with the passage of time and bearing considerable emotional strain that the analyst can find meaning in such a hopeless atmosphere. She might discern that all this had reflected an immersion in the unconscious roles assigned to her by the patient and find a path forward, from within the patient's worldview, to temporarily stand outside of the stuck pattern and move the analysis forward (Chaplan, 2013).

The chronic hopeless countertransference, although difficult to bear, becomes a valuable tool in understanding the patient's inner conflicts and resistances:

> … relentless, prolonged quality of repetitive, "signature" patterns of interaction in the analyses, sometimes leading to the analyst's feeling at wit's end. Relief occurs only when the analyst grasps something preconscious, just beyond the pair's immediate communication … the stuckness morphs into something "the same only slightly different," a sign of growth within the heart of the entanglement. (Chaplan, 2013, p. 593)

The analyst strives to make some meaning of this misery and emptiness, only to find herself often confused and shut out. Amati-Mehler and Argentieri (1989) eloquently speak of this experience:

> With a feeling of weariness, the analyst too analysed her own
> painful sense of frustration, impotence, exasperation and
> irritation; the sense of challenge launched by such overt despair
> and the desire to meet the challenge and to fight the destructive-
> ness of inertia and failure; above all, the authentic sense of com-
> passion for the patient and the wish to understand the sense of
> this stubborn mechanism. It is only through time and consider-
> able emotional strain that the analyst can find meaning in the
> hopeless atmosphere. (p. 296)

A common and surprising aspect of this relentless hopelessness is often
*a secret unspoken and unfelt hopefulness* within the patient (and often
in the analyst as well). Hidden and operating outside of awareness, this
hope lies buried in the bitter heart of the patient's overt hopelessness
(Amati-Mehler & Argentieri, 1989). The stereotyped atmosphere of
despair paradoxically carries a deep unconscious hope: that what was
lost in early (often preverbal) childhood can be regained: "The analysis
and the analyst are invested with an unrealistic task, which consists in
preserving the illusion that what is past or lost forever can still be pro-
vided and restored. The perpetuation of this demand, accompanied by
resentment about the lack of its fulfillment, is the extreme defense against
the threat of separation" (Amati-Mehler & Argentieri, 1989, p. 302).
Danielian and Gianotti (2012) describe this as "loyal waiting," an unconscious idealized solution projected in fantasy onto a longed-for perfect
other to heal wounds from the past. Implicit in the patient's hopelessness
is the message, "I did not get what I deserved in childhood, and I am going
to hold out until I get what is due to me" (Danielian & Gianotti, 2012).

The desperate unconscious longing to regain what has been lost
cancels "realistic hope" and creates a stuck scenario where the patient
and analyst can be bound forever in fantasy. Experiencing genuine hopefulness would mean a catastrophic rupture from this rigid and timeless
fantasy of being united with the idealized lost object from childhood.
Omnipotent hope and hopelessness unite in these moments:

> The paradox lies in the necessity to have both opposites coex-
> ist. There is no alternative intermediary space between how "it
> was" and how "it should be"; pathological hope cancels realis-
> tic hope and gives way to hopelessness. Real chances available

in life are dismissed, or rather not recognized, because they do
not fit the rigid model that illusion pretends to realize ... In fact
... it seems as if the resentment and the mournful complaint
represented the last and unique possible tie with the primary
object, and as if giving this up would mean the definite down-
fall of illusion and the admission that it is really, truly lost. An
interminable analysis thus, as we said before, or even an interminable chain of subsequent analyses, can serve to guarantee
oneself a perfect accomplice to keep this pathological hope alive.
(Amati-Mehler & Argentieri, 1989, p. 302)

In describing these "someday" and "if only" fantasies inherent in unconscious fantasies of hope, Akhtar (1996) notes that the analyst's task is
in helping the patient transition from "pathological" hope to realistic
hope, the danger being a worsening of clinging to the "stuck" pattern of
hopelessness.

It is essential, however, to keep in mind the dialectic inherent in
these "pathological" fantasies: Hopeful fantasies are also privately held
intrapsychically, interpersonally, and as culturally derived "protective illusions" of a particular form of wish and fantasy. As Slochower
(2006) wisely notes, these hopeful illusions can both be a support and
a limitation to clinical work; they can illuminate as well as distort by
opening up the realm of paradox, irony, and fantasy. Hopeful illusions
further the therapeutic process if they are engaged playfully and flu-
idly, existing alongside the nuanced aspects of reality, creating a sense
of protective fantasy that can help both the patient and analyst tolerate
uncertainty and disappointment. It is only when these illusions become
"thick and impenetrable" in the intersubjective space between the analyst and patient that they can be used defensively to avoid the unbearable and unthinkable (Slochower, 2006). It is in this struggle between
hope and hopelessness, between illusion and disillusionment where we
attempt to creatively find a way forward in our work with stuck patients.

## Case example

Beth, a forty-eight-year-old second-generation Iranian-American
librarian with two children, began treatment with me after the
collapse of her marriage of twenty years due to her husband's frequent

violent outbursts and substance abuse. She reported recurrent depressive symptoms, constant anxiety, and chronic difficulties with recurrent muscular pain throughout her upper body and abdomen which had gone undiagnosed and been treated periodically with steroid medications by her rheumatologist. Beth described her past as filled with disappointments and rejections. Beth's mother struggled with psychotic depression throughout her life and died suddenly, isolated and living alone. She felt her mother was distant and critical of her growing up and favored her more attractive younger sister and older brother. Although her father was occasionally experienced as charming and seductive, he was often emotionally absent and had multiple affairs with other women, which confused Beth and left her feeling betrayed.

Highly educated and verbal, Beth was eager to begin psychotherapy and readily agreed to an analysis after several months of treatment with some relief of her symptoms. After two months into the analysis, however, Beth's depression, anxiety, and chronic pain returned with full force and filled her with despair after a romantic disappointment with a man she had met online. She described constant unremitting anxiety and pain, and was unable to obtain any relief from medications. Beth filled the analytic hours with descriptions of her suffering and her anger at her ex-husband for abandoning her, as well as her frustration at others whom she felt could not help her. Any attempts to empathically engage Beth or interpret her hurt and frustration left her feeling more alone and misunderstood. She began to feel hopeless about the analytic process and wondered if it was useful at all. What had started as a promising treatment for Beth now felt dead and lifeless to her. I began to feel a deep sense of despair and hopelessness with Beth that was difficult to bear. Time felt frozen and no sense of growth or change felt possible. A feeling of confusion and unreality took hold of me and I had difficulty understanding what was happening between us. Any moments of genuine reflection or closeness between us quickly eroded into doubts and despair about the process.

After several months of hearing Beth's unremitting agony, a disturbing image of a lifeless corpse in a morgue being beaten over and over again by an anonymous stranger repeatedly entered my mind and stayed with me during these difficult moments. At first thought, I felt the image represented Beth beating me, a dead analyst, over and over again with her hopelessness as an expression of her aggression and envy towards me. Reflecting further, it occurred to me that it was my own anger towards Beth that was being expressed. Perhaps this sadistic fantasy was a way of allowing me some connection with her during moments when I felt completely shut out from her, "beating" some life into our relationship. Regardless of what the image meant, I felt it was important to bear these difficult fantasies and to struggle with empathically staying close to her inner experience despite the worsening deadening atmosphere.

Several sessions after this event, Beth flatly stated being in analysis was like "beating a dead horse," with no hope for any change. She then associated to loving to ride horses when she visited her aunt in Connecticut when she was twelve; there was a feeling of excitement and exhilaration that she lost as an adult. The image of Beth, free and hopeful with excitement resonated with me, but then I suddenly remembered my own image of a stranger beating a dead body, and in Beth's words "beating a dead horse." Was this image of our relationship more comfortable for both of us than a more passionate and exciting experience? It occurred to me that I was distancing myself from Beth. I was surprised to realize that I felt uncomfortable being close to Beth's exhilaration and excitement and my body language and tone of voice reflected this on some level. Perhaps I was experiencing what Beth experienced growing up: helpless and confused, without any relatedness except for beating on what was already dead, an experience of her mother's psychotic withdrawal. However, it also felt as though I was enacting and identifying with the image of her critical and distant mother who felt uncomfortable with being close with Beth, who was creative and full of life as a young child.

These reflections allowed me to somewhat regain my bearings and notice the way in which I colluded with Beth's protection of herself from her longings of intimacy with me. Later in the analysis, she spoke about her chronic hopelessness as a way of embracing her mother's presence, never letting her go. Letting go of her hopelessness in our work together meant letting go of the hope that she could attain some level of intimacy with her unattainable mother that she always dreamed of having, and experiencing the psychic terror of self-annihilation and abandonment without her. Being locked in a hopeless struggle with me preserved this fantasy.

## Hopelessness and frozen time

My experience of hopelessness with Beth also involved a distortion of time. Related to the unconscious fantasies of returning to longed-for experiences of primary union is the countertransference experience of time being frozen. In contrast to the expected ebb and flow of time found in a typical analytic encounter, it feels as though time stands still in these moments. The analyst feels caught in an eternal dead space. The defensive aims of this time standstill include the patient's wish to arrest growth, to avoid change, to postpone adulthood, and to preserve archaic rescue fantasies (Akhtar, 1996; Amati-Mehler & Argentieri, 1989; Orgel, 2012; Wurmser, 2012). The experience of frozen time might also be a method of defending against psychic dissolution and trauma (Giovacchini, 1993; Schmithusen, 2012). This central traumatic experience, which the analyst reexperiences in the countertransference, is a representation of and a defense against an early traumatic situation where time is arrested in the present to avoid being confronted again with the breakdown which occurred in infancy. The patient wards off this primal terror of annihilation (which is unconsciously a part of his experience) by rendering the analyst an inaccessible dead object which results in his experience of time standstill:

> The phenomenon of time standing still is brought about due to a radical defense. Through this phenomenon, defenses are actively brought into play, which prevents any further development of the catastrophic fear that developed when the child was separated from the maternal object at a time before the ego was consolidated. This fear of reexperiencing a traumatic psychic breakdown derives from a severely traumatic experience which took place in the past at a time when the immature psychic apparatus was overwhelmed and internalized … This standstill in time is the result of a defense against an underlying, nonsymbolized and as such incomprehensible fear of annihilation or fear of psychic death, and at the same time it is a precise repetition of this earlier relationship of psychic annihilation that takes place in the transference relationship. The standstill in time is an attempt to deny the reality of circular, cyclic, as well as linear time and therefore to negate development. (Schmithusen, 2012, p. 70)

Introducing the temporal element into the analysis by discussing the passing of years and the end of things (including in some cases the analysis) can lead to a premature retraumatization of the patient. However, if the analyst's holding functions are firmly in place and if sufficient time for mourning has been allowed, then utilizing this countertransference experience for interpretive purposes can deepen the patient's moorings in the temporal dimension of experience and the reality of linear time.

## Reactions to the patient's hopelessness

Reviewing the literature on countertransference reactions to these emotionally challenging clinical scenarios, several common themes emerge. The analyst, feeling the weight of hopelessness and negativity enveloping the analytic space and herself to be difficult to bear, feels an oppressive environment and a need to act or escape. Often these reactions are responses to a disruption of the analyst's sense of self and professional identity or the analytic setting. There is a temporary loss of the observing analytic self, where one's own emotional reactions can be used in the service of deepening the analytic experience for the patient.

Countertransference disturbances usually involve threats to the analyst's professional self-representation, the analyst's mode of operation, and the analytic setting itself (Giovacchini, 1993). A constant bombardment of misery, pessimism, and doubt in the analytic setting feel intrusive and disruptive of the analytic process, even if there are no overt attempts or demands on the patient's part. Unconsciously, the analyst might feel that the patient is not providing the necessary feedback the analyst needs to feel secure in his analytic role, and experiences the patient's hopelessness as an assault on his sense of self and identity. As Giovacchini (1993) notes, "Patients, of course, have no obligation to make their therapists happy or avoid upsetting their narcissistic balance. Nevertheless, analysts are human, and they will react to certain situations regardless of their professional orientation" (p. 162). This painful narcissistic injury can then lead the analyst to defensively protect herself, which can lead to a disruption of the analytic setting. The analyst, unable to bear this injury, feels compelled to either under-respond or over-respond to her internal feelings of misery and despair.

## Under-responsiveness to hopelessness

As described above, intractable narcissistic transferences in patients with melancholia, severe trauma, somatoform disorders, or other narcissistic states can lead to a deadening of the analytic space. The analyst feels bored or pushed aside. The patient's speech and manner of relating create an effect in the analyst that she is not being related to; instead, the analyst feels as if she is an "excluded observer," shut out from relating to the patient (Steiner, 2011a). In these moments, there is a disembodied quality to the analytic space which may be difficult to tolerate. The analyst is tempted to escape from this experience by withdrawing inward. Daydreaming, sleepiness, frequent glances at the clock, allowing the patient to "just keep talking until time runs out" are emotional tactics aimed at managing the hopeless and deadening atmosphere. If sustained, these symptoms can also lead to countertransference dissociation (see Chapter 5 on Dissociation).

These emotional retreats can also be means of expressing hatred towards the patient—an experience that can cause guilt and anxiety if fully felt. In their classic paper on hate and countertransference, Maltsberger and Buie (1974) describe countertransference hate as a mixture of aversion and malice. They argue that the aversive component of hatred is the fundamentally most dangerous because the aversive impulse tempts the therapist to psychologically abandon the patient. Narcissistic transferences, threats of suicide (see Chapter 3 on Dread), and assaults on the analyst's ideal can lead to uncomfortably intense countertransference reactions that are often unconsciously defended against and avoided:

> There is a tendency to daydream about being elsewhere doing something else with someone else. Subjectively, the therapist may be aware of some anxiety and restlessness, or possibly he may find himself drowsy. He may feel bored. While this defense offers little scope for acting out of the unconscious or preconscious hostility, the therapist may well convey his aversion to the patient by yawning, glancing too often and too obviously at his clock, or by other signs of inattention, conveying nonverbally to his patient, "I do not want to be with you." (p. 639)

These emotional retreats can turn into covert and secretive hostile attacks on listening to the patient. Slochower (2006) describes these moments as "the analyst's secret delinquencies," which are ways in which we exploit an opportunity to withdraw emotionally or cognitively from our patients, and by doing so privately violate our professional ethics. Slochower describes numerous examples of these delinquent acts, including writing notes to oneself, adding to a grocery list, planning an event, checking email, cutting sessions short by a few minutes, charging for a missed session without explicit warning or discussion with the patient, taking phone calls during a session, or eating meals with the patient. These "minor acts of psychopathy" on the part of the analyst are often painfully discordant with their analytic ideal self, which results in a "quasi-conscious disavowal" of the breach on both the analyst's and patient's part (Slochower, 2006, p. 71). Here the work of the analyst is to tolerate the shame and the disruption of her professional self image and create more of a space to address these moments and the underlying feelings that have motivated these actions.

Another method of avoiding a direct experience of hatred in these difficult clinical circumstances is the analyst turning hate against herself and having fantasies of self-devaluation and degradation. Chronic doubt, feelings of worthlessness, and hopelessness in the analyst can serve as "masochistic retreats" away from the patient and a direct experience of frustration and hatred towards the patient, which could render the analyst with feelings of unbearable guilt and shame. This turning inward can then be interpreted as a rejection from the patient, which can lead to further defensiveness and acting out.

## Over-reactiveness to hopelessness

The analytic attitude of free floating attention to both the patient's transferences and the analyst's own countertransference reactions can be put in jeopardy when the analysis feels like it is in a hopeless quagmire of deadness and doubt. In my experience, this usually begins with an uncomfortable feeling of helplessness in our ability to understand or be useful, which often is only vaguely felt in the clinical moment. This bypassed and often unregistered helplessness in the analyst over time gives way to a hopelessness in an analysis that feels stuck or lifeless.

Helplessness in the present moment grinds itself into a hopeless stalemate about the possibility of growth and change for the future.

In this chronic unbearable state, the analyst, overcome with hopelessness and doubt, can feel the temptation to "do something." Often this impulse is not fully felt by the analyst until it is satisfied. One might have certitude in one's convictions which feel hurried, or a certain pressure in one's body to act or perform some task for the patient. Giovacchini (1993) describes this experience well:

> The therapist feels confused and anxious because he does not understand what is going on … he feels helpless and frustrated and is overcome by an impulse to do something. He struggles, out of his anxiety, to give himself and the patient relief … the function of interpretation in these difficult circumstances is not to expand understanding … rather, the interpretation is designed to make the analyst feel better and to halt the patient's protestations and manifestations of psychopathology … the patient, instead of feeling understood, only senses and receives the anxious parts of the interpretation. (p. 30)

Of historical note, Hinshelwood (2013) argues that this type of countertransference may have occurred in Freud's (1918b) treatment of Sergei Pankejeff, given the pseudonym "Wolf Man": frustrated by his "obliging apathy," lack of self-sufficiency, and passivity, "Freud was provoked to take action on the basis of the emotional state of frustration … having been provoked, Freud's irritation and impatience led him to become active" (p. 91).

Subjectively, the analyst in the moment of giving the interpretation often feels a firm sense of conviction and certitude; it is only on later reflection that she realizes the defensive nature of the interpretation. Britton and Steiner (1994) refer to this phenomenon as an *overvalued idea* on the part of the analyst. They describe the experience of conviction in the analyst as often inaccurate and at times mistaken. These "overvalued ideas" are due to the defensive needs of the analyst: "The experience of a moment of insight or discovery may give a sense of excitement and achievement to the analyst" (Britton & Steiner, 1994, p. 1070). However, once uttered, the insight often loses some of its conviction and "the importance of doubt, guilt and other feelings associated with the depressive position" become conscious in the analyst (p. 1070). Being aware of the possibility that our understanding may serve our own defensive agenda allows us to be cautious and sustain doubt, which necessitates us observing the therapeutic process to ascertain if our interpretations and insights are helpful to the therapeutic process.

Unfelt helplessness that gives way to hopelessness in the analyst can also lead to defensive certainty in one's therapeutic actions which in retrospect feel forced or one-dimensional. Steiner (2011b), in his paper, "Helplessness and the Exercise of Power in the Analytic Session," describes this phenomenon as "narcissistic helpfulness." Rapid interpretations given with a degree of certainty (see Chapter 1 on Arrogance) and a quickening pace can be a clue that this type of "helpfulness" is operating in the analytic space. The aim of the intervention by the analyst unconsciously is not to deepen the analytic process, but to give the analyst and patient relief from the unbearable experience that has occurred between them, often involving a state of complete helplessness and vulnerability which leads to hopelessness. As Steiner notes:

> My over-activity concealed an inner feeling of helplessness. I could see that I was colluding with the patient's phantasm of omnipotent repair and that I too had been trying to prevent a disaster and restore the patient to reason. It then became possible for me to admit to myself that I could not protect the patient from his acting out, and my feeling of helplessness gave way to sadness … once I accepted my helplessness, I seemed to be able to be more thoughtful. (2011b, p. 126)

Steiner goes on to say that narcissistic helpfulness is rarely successful because it ignores the actual needs of the object. It also involves a concrete type of thinking in which the object has to be materially restored, and as a result it betrays omnipotent fantasy rather than genuine reparation.

This defensive reaction on the part of the analyst is often experienced in the treatment of trauma survivors. Defending against the unbearable sense of helplessness felt with the patient, the therapist unconsciously attempts to assume the role of the omnipotent rescuer (Herman, 1992). These temptations also exist in analyzing the patient's pathologically "hopeful" early childhood fantasies of union and symbiosis. There may be an urge to rescue the patient, colluding with the omnipotent fantasy, or actively interpreting the defenses too quickly in an effort to ward off one's own unfelt hopelessness. As Akhtar (1996) notes:

> The analyst must be highly vigilant toward his own emotional experience. The informative potential of countertransference in such cases is considerable. Since the idealization inherent in "someday" and "if only" fantasies is not easily verbalized by the patient, often the analyst has to decipher it through his own feelings. Within transference, the analyst is invested by these patients with the task of preserving an illusion. This puts pressure on the analyst. On the one hand, there is the temptation to actively rescue the patient. On the other hand, there is the allure of quickly showing the patient that his expectations are unrealistic, and serve defensive aims. Cloaked in the guise of therapeutic zeal, hasty attempts of this sort often emanate from the analyst's own unresolved narcissism and infantile omnipotence. (p. 743)

The quickening pace of one's experience with the patient and the urge to act are often clues to this process of "narcissistic helpfulness" occurring in the analytic space. There is a concrete zeal and excitement about "figuring it out" or "finally getting to something important" that can be intoxicating because it eliminates the dreadful hopeless atmosphere pervading the relationship. Allowing oneself to recognize this unbearable hopelessness can pave the path towards a richer and more nuanced perspective.

## Case example

Judy, a fifty-six-year-old second-generation Mexican American school teacher, entered psychoanalytic psychotherapy to treat her long-standing severe depressive symptoms which increased after her husband began questioning their relationship because of a lack of strength and passivity he perceived on Judy's part. She felt these comments "destroyed" her because she was already feeling a profound sense of inadequacy and shame about her inability to return to work after taking twelve years off to raise their two boys. The victim of sexual abuse by her stepfather, Julie decided to dedicate her life to her children to allow them to feel safe and protected in a way she never felt. As her two boys grew up, she found herself feeling less and less involved in their daily life and finding herself more isolated and alone. This led to a return of painful ruminations of recurrent self-blame and criticism, which she felt she had previously liberated herself from. Judy reported desperately wanting to go back to work and felt it was imperative that we set this as our goal for treatment. As the therapy progressed, Judy felt her symptoms of depression decreased and she was more able to engage with her husband and her children. Despite this, she felt a profound inhibition to engage in any work. Any effort to help Judy understand her conflicts around returning to teaching would lead to a concrete pattern: She desperately wanted to return to work, but "simply" could not bring herself to do it.

After one year of treatment, I began to feel a sense of hopelessness about Judy's situation. Despite her reporting decreased guilt and distress, she had made no progress in returning to work and continued to insist it was the most important aspect of her progress. Feeling a sense of urgency about her situation, I found myself eagerly and quickly making interpretations that felt satisfying to me at the moment of speaking them—it was as if I was eagerly trying to solve the puzzle of her obvious conflict over teaching. I began to make genetic interpretations involving her conflicts with competitiveness and power and her difficulty with bearing the loss of safety her current life offered, with an assuredness that felt forced in retrospect. These interpretations led to her feeling more confused and wanting a behavioral solution to her problems, with Judy remarking with exasperation, "I wish someone would just push me to do it." Reflecting on this enactment, I realized that I was carrying an unfelt sense of hopelessness that was leading me to be overly active and helpful, playing the role of the omnipotent rescuer. This allowed me to regain a more calm and reflective stance which then led to a space for a shared feeling of helplessness which had echoes of her early sexual trauma, where she felt coerced and frightened into submission.

This movement to more concrete thinking on the part of the analyst can also be seen in situations where the analyst, desperate to find some relief, begins to formulate in her mind and relate to the patient in a more "practical" and concrete fashion. Problem-solving or other alternatives to the analysis, such as psychopharmacology, take center stage in the analyst's vision of treatment. While it is true that these other modalities of treatment can be incredibly useful and important aspects of therapy and should certainly be taken into consideration, the impulse on the part of the analyst to move in this direction in her thinking about the patient should warrant some self-reflection. (Of note, the impulse not to consider other modalities of treatment are also worthy of reflection, especially when the analysis is at a stalemate.)

Giovacchini (1993) notes that in "hopeless" clinical situations, the therapist will try to give something therapeutically helpful to the patient, but the patient cannot accept or use what is being offered at the time. This in turn is felt as a narcissistic blow by the therapist, who by offering medication or a concrete treatment plan can then be cast in the role of omnipotent savior, restoring the therapist's narcissistic supplies: "The therapist's knowledge of and capacity to prescribe drugs is exalted … they [the therapists] can maintain their narcissistic equilibrium as they identity with the powerful, potentially magical, curative effect of the antidepressant drugs" (Giovacchini, 1993, p. 282). This in turn can lead to a withdrawal from the patient's inner life and conflicts and lead to a deadening of the analytic environment.

If the analyst cannot feel they can "reach" the patient, or if they feel despite their best efforts their patients are not improving, hopelessness in the countertransference can begin to give way to aggression and sadism. The forbidden delight of analysts resorting to sadomasochistic enactments with patients, both subtle and overt, is a difficult and guilt-provoking reality. It is worth noting several subtle enactments that may take place in this regard. Using language or a tone of speech that conveys criticism of a patient's inner life can inadvertently occur, as well as taking a harsh, overly parental attitude with the patient. While a healthy sense of humor and playfulness often deepen an analysis, using humor in a subtly mocking fashion towards the patient may also be a method of discharging tension and anger.

Analysis is certainly not an easy task, for the patient or analyst. In order for the analysis to deepen and for psychic change to occur, the unbearable aspects of one's inner experience need to be contended with within the analytic space. The analyst's ability to have the capacity to tolerate and contain what feels unrelenting and unbearable without defensively "colonizing" the patient with her own perspective or personality is essential (Ferro, 2002). When this occurs, the experience of hopelessness within the analyst can surprisingly be a fertile space where growth can occur despite its seemingly bleak exterior. Once the concrete and rigid internal experience of hopelessness is ruptured in the analyst, a more textured perspective emerges.

Tenacious hopelessness surprisingly intertwines with clinging to longed-for hopeful reunions, and psychic deadness breathes for new life and a hunger for vitality. Frozen endless time can be glimpsed as a longing for union and timelessness. These experiences are true for both the analyst and analysand, who by engaging in the analytic space risk the emotional storm of intimacy that hopelessness can stand against.

# CHAPTER 8

# Jealousy

*Jealousy, that dragon which slays love under the pretence of keeping it alive.*

—Havelock Ellis

To experience jealousy is to experience mental torture. Jealousy feels visceral and urgent, pressing for action or relief. One literally feels torn up inside, imprisoned in a cage of longing and exclusion. Searing hot-blooded psychic pain combined with unrelenting desire feels unbearable and excruciating. Jealousy does not have the advantage of being an experience that feels noble or moral. In fact, it is quite the reverse—it feels shameful and filled with hatred. Roland Barthes (1977) describes it well:

> As a jealous person, I suffer fourfold: because I am jealous, because I reproach myself for my jealousy, because I fear that my jealousy is hurting the other, because I allow myself to be enslaved by banality: I suffer from being excluded, from being aggressive, from being crazy, and from being common. (p. 146)

The dreaded consequences of jealousy surround us: Old and new stories of jealous lovers murdering and committing unspeakable acts of cruelty are commonplace, from reality television shows to the ancient myths of Greece. Jealousy haunts all of us—as Freud (1922b) wrote, "Jealousy is one of those affective states … that may be described as normal. If anyone appears to be without it, the inference is justified that it has undergone severe repression and consequently plays all the greater part in his unconscious mental life" (p. 223).

Despite this ubiquity, our experiences of jealousy as psychoanalysts and psychotherapists are not readily discussed, with a few notable exceptions including Searles (1986), Lewin (2011), and Wurmser and Jarass (2008a). This is especially curious considering the centrality of the experience of jealousy in psychoanalytic theorizing, foremost in the oedipal struggles of childhood and the intense rivalries and passions between parents and children that need to be confronted and mourned. As the Freud quote above states, jealousy is a fundamental experience in every person's life and childhood. For it to be missing indicates it has "gone underground," banished from consciousness.

One could argue that perhaps it has to do with the emotional discomfort over our experience of jealousy, but this does not feel sufficient. Envy and sadism are obviously very disruptive and difficult emotions for us to bear in the analytic setting but have been discussed more openly and in detail. The central argument of this chapter is to make the case that jealousy is indeed an emotional experience that is especially difficult for an analyst to come to terms with because of its unique qualities that differentiate it from other negative emotional experiences. Specifically, jealousy always involves a third object—real or imagined (or both).

Psychoanalysis and psychoanalytic psychotherapy is at its core a two-person experience: In a private setting, apart from the rest of the world, we are with our patients in a passionate yet controlled setting. The experience of jealousy disrupts this primordial peaceful Eden for both the patient and the therapist, reminding them both of their shock of learning that whoever we love and imagine we possess has others in their life: mothers, fathers, real and imagined lovers—an internal "secret garden" that we can never fully be a part of (Britton, 1998). We are all excluded from paradise.

To avoid this shock, it is tempting to "coast" in a two-person experience without dealing with the complexity of this triadic experience (Hirsch, 2008). The analyst can feel she is in a privileged role of being the exclusive caregiver to someone in need, an experience from early in childhood prior to the discovery and shock of the third represented in the primal scene. This avoids the narcissistic blow to omnipotence that occurs when we discover the person we love most has others in their lives they love, possibly (terribly) more.

The importance of the analytic setting being a holding environment and a place of safety in order for the process to unfold may unwittingly be what also conveniently allows us not to experience jealousy with our patients consciously. The analyst's careful listening to unconscious themes in the manifest material, and allowing herself to be affected and tuned in to his patient's free associations and subtle or unstated emotional experiences, deepens the dyadic experience for both parties. The more powerful the experience, the greater the risk of jealousy for both the patient and the analyst when the inevitable truth of triadic reality occurs. The analyst, however, is at risk in a particular way because of her need to be both intimately involved with the patient and also respectful of the patient's boundaries.

Unconscious jealousy on the part of the analyst can lead to possessiveness, seductiveness, and a rupture of boundaries or a stalemate in treatment. If the analyst is able to bear the onslaught of jealousy in the treatment and use this experience to understand the patient's experience, however, a movement towards triadic reality can occur within the analytic space, and the patient can begin to learn the difficult task of balancing exclusivity and sharing, loving without total possession (Wurmser & Jarass, 2008a).

## Defining jealousy

Prior to exploring the analyst's experiences of jealousy, it would be worthwhile to first explore the experience of jealousy in more depth. Psychoanalysts have viewed jealousy as a primary emotional experience that can be conscious or unconscious (Wurmser & Jarass, 2008a). Others have highlighted jealousy as a defense against other affective states, including envy (Riviere, 1932), guilt (Wurmser & Jarass, 2008a), emptiness (Blevis, 2006), or a defense against intimacy (Coen, 1987). Freud originally described jealousy as an affective state with three layers: competitive, or "normal" jealousy, projected jealousy, and delusional jealousy. Interestingly, Freud (1922b) was quick to bypass "normal jealousy":

> There is not much to be said from the analytic point of view about normal jealousy. It is easy to see that essentially it is compounded of grief, the pain caused by the thought of losing the loved object, and the narcissistic wound, in so far as this is distinguishable from the other wound; further, of feelings of enmity against the successful rival, and of a greater or lesser amount of self-criticism which tries to hold the person himself accountable for his loss. Although we may call it normal this jealousy is by no means completely rational, that is, derived from the actual situation, proportionate to the real circumstances and under the complete control of the conscious ego; for it is rooted deep in the unconscious, it is a continuation of the earliest stirrings of the child's affective life and it originates in the Oedipus or family complex of the first sexual period. (p. 221)

What Freud stated as "easy to see," even in Freud's in-depth description, is emotionally complex from an experiential point of view. This chapter will focus on this "normal" jealousy, consciously and unconsciously experienced by the analyst. Why was Freud so quick to bypass "normal jealousy"? It is known that Freud considered himself a jealous person and his theorizing of the jealous rivalry in the Oedipus complex was motivated by his own self analysis (Baumgart, 1990). Psychoanalytic historians have also noted Freud's intense jealous rivalries with others in his inner circle (Makari, 2008). Perhaps Freud himself was uncomfortable with this especially torturous emotional experience.

Regardless of the reasons for doing so, Freud may have unwittingly minimized the complex and unique qualities of the experience of "normal" jealousy for the analyst. Unlike other affective states, jealousy involves emotions involving three people, not two: the lover, the beloved, and the rival. Jealousy is a complex brew. Towards the rival, one feels varying degrees of hatred, envy, admiration, and competitiveness.

Jealousy induces complex feelings towards the beloved as well, including unbearable longing, intense grief, and psychic pain over the loss of love, rage over being replaced, and guilt over this hatred. Narcissistic injury, helplessness, and the shame of exclusion accompanied by self-criticism are acutely felt as well (Akhtar, 2009; Auchincloss & Samberg, 2012).

Importantly, the jealous individual is tortured by being simultaneously included and excluded—it is essentially an "inside out" experience symbolized by the primal scene. Because of his desire he is on the "inside" longing painfully for his beloved, while simultaneously being "outside," excluded by a rival his beloved prefers: "Ravaged, yet burned with desire, he errs endlessly in jealousy's labyrinth, incapable of finding an exit" (Blevis, 2006, p. 3). There are no gray areas in the experience of jealousy; emotionally it is a zero sum game: "You love him, not me—I am nothing to you." As Wurmser and Jarass (2008a) note, jealousy "involves a regression to strictly oedipal states of mind such that the object of desire and the rival are felt to be more intact, powerful, and sexually flourishing than is the jealous self, which is experienced as weak, inadequate, and desperately dependent on the love of the desired object and often of the rival as well" (p. 32).

## Jealousy and the triadic experience

Underlying the experience of jealousy is a secret hope of exclusivity and possessiveness: "At its core, there is a sheltered ... the fantasy of an all-powerful twosome unity from which everybody else, even the entire world, should be banished ... the essence of jealousy lies in this absoluteness and exclusivity of the demanded relationship" (Wurmser & Jarass, 2008c, p. 5). Attachment research has demonstrated jealous responses as early as early as four months old (Hart et al., 2004). Hart et al. argue that the loss of exclusiveness represents momentary disrupted attachment, and the infant's expression of jealousy through expressions of emotions such as sadness functions to solicit caregiving: "Jealousy protest signifies the meaningfulness of the attachment relationship" (p. 72). Interestingly, the level of intensity of attachment to the mother predicted the jealous response, a finding that will be discussed later in this chapter on the analyst's emerging awareness of her jealousy as the relationship with the patient deepens.

The fantasy of a return to a "twosome unity" of an exclusive relationship to avoid triadic reality is discussed in every psychoanalytic tradition. The idealization of a merger with a powerful and loving caregiver, a "completeness that closes in on itself" (Lacan, 1973, p. 116) is an extremely powerful one, warding off the horror of separateness and loss. The shock of a child learning that his beloved mother, his everything, is involved with others (often represented by and symbolized as father) is a crushing experience for the child.

This defeat forces him to realize one can no longer retain a claim of omnipotence to the desire of the other: "The discovery of the oedipal triangle is felt to be the death of the couple ... in this phantasy the arrival of the notion of the third always murders the dyadic relationship" (Britton, 1998, p. 37). It is here where jealousy finds its origins, in the moment of realization of a third, a moment of exclusion from the comfort and safety of the loving dyadic union:

> In jealousy I feel: I am the one who has been excluded from love. I am standing outside of an intimate relationship that is particularly precious to me. Behind jealousy, there is always a sense of loss, and with that, acute pain and sadness, but also a feeling of humiliation and shame ... I am the excluded third and want to be the excluding first ... I am excluded from belonging ... and my pain and shame are so strong that I want to hurl myself against this exclusion, but feel helpless to do anything about it. (Wurmser & Jarass, 2008b, p. xi)

It is important to note here that the essential pain of jealousy and exclusion is not merely the fear of losing the lost object. The core feature of jealousy is the torture of bearing witness to the fact that the person you desire is desiring and enjoying pleasure with someone else without you—the fantasy of blissful twoness collapses. As Benvenuto (2016) notes,

> The subject [of jealousy] is outside the scene—"I am a source of neither desire nor enjoyment to the others whom I love" ... in jealousy, the sense of exclusion is overturned by the sensation that a third party is irremediably included in the relationship

of the couple; and that third party, which excludes me, is always including itself in my erotic relationship. (pp. 13–14)

In contrast to envy, which is a malignant and hateful attack on something valued and good that another person possesses, jealousy is by definition a triadic and complex experience based in exclusion. It should be added, however, that jealousy is not a more "mature" and less regressive emotion than envy: the murderousness and blind rage in a jealous betrayal are well known to all of us.

These varied experiences of jealousy can be recreated and reenacted on the analytic stage between analyst and analysand, both participating in a fantasied dyadic relationship. The "arrival of the notion of the third" is always looming, threatening to disrupt the happy couple at any time:

> When we claim to be one of the "happy pair" we rid ourselves by projection of that aspect of ourselves which is forever "unfilled with the pain of longing" and with it we project our potential for envy and jealousy ... clinically, this is familiar and frequent in analysis in various intensities. (Britton, 1998, p. 124)

## The emergence of acute conscious jealousy in the analyst

There is an absence of a detailed discussion on the topic of the analyst's experience of jealousy in the psychoanalytic literature, with one notable exception: Harold Searles. In a series of intriguing and boldly honest chapters (Searles, 1986), he describes the experience of jealousy in the analyst and its therapeutic possibilities in depth.

Searles viewed the experience of jealousy as inevitable for both analyst and patient alike and described his own struggles with jealousy in a manner that would be difficult even for the contemporary analyst well versed in the importance of putting words to countertransference experiences. He also noted that his conscious experiences of being jealous of patients grew as the treatment deepened, and felt the experience of jealousy in the analyst heralded the opportunity to understand the patient's jealousy in an in-depth manner. The experience of jealousy in the countertransference emotionally communicates to the analyst the experience of the patient's struggles which he is not yet conscious of, as this case illustrates.

## Case example

Deven was a twenty-seven-year-old adopted Sri Lankan computer engineer with a history of depression and difficulty in maintaining long-lasting relationships with women. He began analysis because of a personal academic interest in psychoanalytic theory and was eager to start on the couch four times a week. As the analysis progressed past a year, it became clear that Deven loved to use obsessional and intellectualized language that intrigued me yet kept me at arm's length. Conceptual insight came readily to both of us and Deven seemed pleased with our relationship and his newfound understanding of himself.

Despite these "insights," nothing really appeared to be changing in his life; his mood remained low, he struggled completing his work, and his interest in pursuing any romantic interest waned even further. In the sessions, although his enthusiasm appeared to continue, it seemed the analysis was an analysis in name only—all of the motions and procedures were in place but there was a lack of depth and relatedness despite our fondness for one another. It was as if there was a barrier we could not cross together. I could not feel his presence with me in any sustained meaningful way—it was as if he did not leave any impact on me, despite the fact that I thought about him often and struggled to feel closer to him. Any discussions about these experiences between us led to further theorizing and conceptual understandings but no meaningful change.

Towards the beginning of his second year of analysis, Deven took me by surprise with the following announcement—he had decided to cut back his analytic sessions, perhaps even terminate temporarily. He had discovered a psychotherapist, Rose, who practiced mindfulness meditation and yoga. She had been encouraging him to end his analysis and start a two-month intensive mind–body workshop with her. Deven spoke about her in a surprisingly tender and passionate fashion and said that he felt "truly and fully" understood by her—I could feel for the first time a true longing in Deven for some type of contact that went beyond theories and ideas. I felt my heart racing and my face flushed—an acute sense of loss gripped my abdomen, and, although it took me some time to consciously face it, I was jealous.

In response, I offered some rambling thoughts about the benefits of mindfulness and therapy, which I now see as a way of me desperately trying to include myself in his newfound interest which felt too painful to be excluded from. This also continued the typical intellectualized intimacy we both found safe. Deven reassured me that the analysis was indeed helpful but he didn't feel it was reaching him at the level Rose did. He found her presence warm and inviting. "She brings out something in me I can't put into words—it's as if she intuitively knows me and understands how to draw me out." The discomfort over my jealousy increased hearing these words—I realized that I wished I had the powers Rose did to bring him to life.

With some reservations, Deven continued the analysis and also decided to see Rose for mindfulness meditation training as well. Although it took some time, over the course of the analysis after this point, the jealousy I felt over being excluded from Deven and Rose had important roots in Deven's childhood experience. My jealousy resonated with a deep feeling of exclusion and shame Deven felt growing up in his household. Adopted at the age of two by a wealthy Irish Catholic family with no siblings, Deven grew up feeling profoundly different from his adopted family, whom he felt were "more guardians than parents." He especially felt a profound mismatch with his mother—coming from a strict and abusive household, Deven's adoptive mother had difficulty with being playful or genuinely affectionate with him. He did feel a great deal of love for his father who encouraged his intellectual passions and abilities, but felt their relationship ended there. One aspect of Deven's experience that was not fully conscious, which emerged in the analysis after my experience of jealousy, were powerful feelings of exclusion and jealousy from both of his parents as a couple.

Deven's parents were childhood lovers and spent all of their time together running a business. They were both in their forties when they adopted Deven, and he often felt excluded from their "inner circle." Reflecting on the first year of the analysis, I realized that the lack of spontaneity and relatedness in our relationship together (which we both contributed to) mirrored his situation growing up with his distant mother and cerebral father. The acute jealousy I experienced upended my role as an emotionally distant parent to a more primal experience of Deven as a young boy excluded from a couple that shared a special bond together. Using this experience as a guide allowed Deven and me to begin to explore his need to protect himself from intimacy to avoid the possible repetition of shame and exclusion that he experienced as a child.

My feelings of acute jealousy that broke through my defenses around keeping Deven emotionally distant from me involved a rival, a "third" that interrupted a fantasised dyadic union between us. My experiences of jealousy towards Rose allowed for a deepening of my understanding of Deven's own experience of exclusion and jealousy he felt throughout his life. While Rose was an actual person in Deven's life that heralded these experiences in our treatment, strangely enough jealousy can also occur intrapsychically between parts of oneself and the analysand.

## The analyst's jealousy of internal objects

Although Searles was one the first to acknowledge the presence of acute conscious jealous feelings in the analyst and their usefulness in understanding the patient's often unconscious emotional experience, he went several steps further in his understanding of jealousy in the analyst, which are surprising but clinically useful. His major contribution is the concept of jealousy occurring intrapsychically between a person's internal objects—an internal jealousy of a part of one's own self. Searles felt this type of jealousy "is a major factor in maintaining the disharmony of the [patient's] internal object world and in preventing him from experiencing a single, whole and continuous identity" (1986, p. 100).

Simplified, the dilemma is as follows: Growing up, the patient experienced the parent narcissistically and passionately involved with one aspect of the patient's existence, such as his body, his intellect, or his ideal (from the past or in the future). This creates dissociation in the patient's experience of this aspect of himself which he then feels jealous of—it is as if the parent and this aspect of the patient have a love affair that the patient is excluded from:

> The patient comes to realize that he is not after all at the center of
> the life of a mother or father who had appeared selflessly devoted

to him ... he now realizes the parent's interest was essentially narcissistic and that, to the extent that he has been a truly separate
person at all to the parent—the parent loves an image of the child
that the child is jealous of. (p. 116)

The analyst's role is to allow herself to become actively engaged with
the patient to the point where she begins to be conscious of feelings of
jealousy that the patient has been previously unconscious of via projective identification. By doing so the analyst can then begin to help the
patient become aware of and integrate this aspect of themselves.

This intrapsychic jealousy that occurs in the analyst can take many
forms in the analyst's countertransference. Searles describes being
excluded and jealous of his patient's preoccupations with hallucinations,
jealous of an idealized image of Searles that the patient seems to be enamored with; even jealous of a man's lavish preoccupation with his penis:

> The analyst finds to his astonishment that he is feeling jealous as
> regards to the patient's intimate and fascinated relationship with
> the latter's own penis. The analyst, that is, first comes to feel as his
> own the jealousy which the patient himself has dissociated for so
> many years, jealousy referable to his mother's relationship with
> his penis. (1986, p. 105)

This strange type of intrapsychic jealousy is best illustrated by Searles's
descriptions of patients' jealousy of their own bodies or body parts. Searles describes to his surprise feeling jealous of his patient's constant focus
(positive or critical) on a particular body part, for example as stated
above a man's penis or a woman's legs, and realizing that the jealousy he
is feeling mirrors an internal jealousy on the part of the patient:

> It is inherent in the successful analyzing of this "intrapsychic"
> jealousy that the analyst become able to experience it vis a vis
> the relationship between the patient and the body parts in ques-
> tion, before the patient can be expected to become aware of, and
> integrate, the strangely jealousy-ridden relationship between her-
> self and one or another introject represented by the body parts in
> question. (p. 105)

The analyst first comes to feel as his own the jealousy which the patient himself has dissociated from childhood, a jealousy of a caregiver's focus on that aspect of the patient's body.

Clinically, this is often seen in patients with eating disorders and body image distortions—a parent's exclusive focus on a child's body image or particular aspect of a child's body becomes idealized. The child then feels a dissociated separateness from their body, as if their body existed in the third person. They often measure them, abuse them, or speak about their bodies as an almost separate entity as if they do not inhabit them (Schwartz & Ceaser, 2005). As a patient, who was a successful athlete, once noted about her mother: "She loved my body but not my soul." This aspect of the patient, her body, could never feel fully lived in and owned, and be a source of pleasure or sexuality. Unconsciously the body belongs to her parent. It is in the analyst's experience of jealousy over being excluded from this body image that the patient is fixated on that unlocks this internal rivalry between the imagined parent, body, and patient.

In a similar fashion, Searles also discusses feeling excluded and jealous of his patient's idealized images of him—one patient imagines his tanned and sculpted body at the beach; another constantly admires his writing but appears to devalue Searles's actual presence: "I experienced uncomfortable stirrings of jealousy of the relatively admired author Searles whose works this scornful man was sure I could not have possibly written" (1986, p. 108). Searles was able to trace these jealous experiences to his patient's early experiences of having a caregiver love an idealized image of the patient either in the future or the past, preferring this image over the actual patient as a person. The jealousy the analyst feels towards the patient's possession of her idealized image reflects a similar jealousy the patient feels towards his own internalized ideal that he imagines he is excluded from: "That experience with her [sic: Searles's patient] left me well able to believe that similar jealousy was mobilized within her on occasions when she sensed that I was visualizing her as being a capable person" (p. 116). This unconscious internal jealous struggle leads the patient to feel excluded and not integrated with his ideal which can lead to a negative therapeutic reaction.

## The analyst's jealousy of inanimate objects

Another interesting and surprising insight Searles discusses is the patient's and therapist's jealous reaction to inanimate objects. Searles (1986) gives vivid descriptions of his patient's feeling jealous over "things" the analyst possesses, including the analyst's chair, desk, and even the office plant. Conversely, the analyst also may experience jealousy of objects patients are enamored with that the analyst feels excluded from. Clinically, the analyst can experience this unusual type of jealous reaction to patients who use drugs, as this case illustrates:

## Case example

John, a twenty-eight-year-old chemical engineer, began treatment for depression and chronic marijuana use. At the urging of his increasingly frustrated wife, John attempted a variety of treatments for his marijuana use and low mood that he described as failures, in part because he felt disengaged with "the annoying self-help mantras" of the therapists he worked with. Despite his struggles with depression and chronic marijuana use, John functioned highly at work and was dedicated to his job. Despite his numerous successes at work, John struggled also with his feelings of low self-worth and a constant feeling of being undervalued and disrespected. He felt isolated from his wife whom he described as constantly irritable and demanding of his attention and time. John did not feel close to anyone in his life—he found himself uncomfortable in most social situations and preferred to be alone in his own thoughts. In his initial sessions with me, John often appeared bored and disengaged, focusing on his disappointments with his colleagues at work and his wife who he complained was demanding and constantly "nagging him."

After several sessions like these I found myself struggling to find some area where John felt alive. I noticed that he never spoke about his marijuana use in detail, only discussing it as a "thing that my wife wants out of my life and I need to stop." I commented on his lack of interest in speaking to me about what it was like for him to smoke marijuana. He replied flatly, "Do you really want to know, or are you asking me so you can figure out how to get me to stop?" I replied that it seemed there was a part of him that wanted me to really know what it was like for him but he assumed I would play the part of others in his life that wanted him to stop.

Over the course of the next several months, John slowly began to describe his passion for cultivating and growing marijuana in the basement of the old family home where his parents still lived after retirement. He would carefully study the art of horticulture online and plant a variety of different species, picking the right soil, carefully paying attention to the pH and the quality of the nutrients in the plants. He would then harvest and "cure" the buds, preparing them for his use. He grew animated discussing this process and I found myself at first fascinated and taken in by the process.

As time went on and our relationship deepened, however, I began to find myself annoyed when he brought up the plants again. It seemed any time we made progress in him being able to speak truthfully about his experience to me, the next session would turn to his "secret garden." In these moments I imagined what his plants looked like and how tenderly he probably cared for them. I began to interrupt his reveries about horticulture with questions about the effects of this hobby on his daily life and his relationship with others, including myself and his wife. His affect shifted and he began to show up late to sessions which increased my feelings of frustration at his lack of interest in our work together— something he would never do to those precious plants of his, I imagined with annoyance!

This thought surprised me and allowed me to realize that I was jealous of John's relationship with his plants, a feeling that I was certain John's wife had as well. An insight occurred to me about John's past that felt relevant but only emerged as emotionally meaningful later in treatment: John's mother suffered from anorexia nervosa and spent hours when John was a child weighing herself in her bathroom with the door locked. Feeling shut out of being able to be with his mother and his jealousy of her constant preoccupation with her body and not him was enacted in my jealous feelings of him being with his marijuana plants when our relationship began to deepen.

John's preoccupation with his marijuana plants is a reminder of our continuous involvement with "things" in our lives that are deeply meaningful to us and the constructive, sustaining, and symbolic significance of the inanimate world (Akhtar, 2003). In addictions, inanimate objects like John's fascination with his plants can take on especially powerful meanings. These include the symbolized lack of felt human connection, the need for control, and the need to use physical objects to ward off mental pain and anguish: "Addictions make psychic pain bearable. Beautiful objects make the addiction bearable" (p. 17).

Allowing myself to examine my own jealous reactions to John's absorption with his marijuana plants led us to be able to speak to his unbearable jealousy towards his mother's preoccupation with her body and his feeling of exclusion from her. While the conscious experience of jealousy for the analyst is obviously disrupting and uncomfortable, if reflected on and mentalized it can serve as a potential guide to understanding. There are also significant dangers of not attending to a powerful emotion.

## Chronic and unconscious jealous countertransference dilemmas

While emerging acute, conscious, jealous feelings in the analyst can lead to a deepening of the analytic experience, chronic unconscious jealousy on the part of the analyst can lead to either impasses or seductive acting out behaviors. As stated above, based on the frame and nature of her work with patients, the analyst is placed in a position that makes her especially prone to jealousy. Despite being actively involved and hearing the patient's most intimate details and fantasies, the analyst is also excluded from fully participating in the unfolding intimacy—her responsiveness and engagement are in the service of the understanding and helping the patient, not for pure gratification.

The analyst is actively engaged and simultaneously excluded from fully participating in this passionate encounter; she is both "inside and out." This can lead to a peculiar type of isolation and loneliness. Being lonely in the company of others is fertile ground for unbearable jealousy. Searles (1986), in his honest and endearing way, states this clearly:

> It should be seen that the loneliness, in reality, of the analyst's work is such to make him highly prey to feeling reality based

jealousy in the analytic setting. The lonely nature of one's work as an analyst is an immensely powerful reality factor which tends to require one to repress the feelings of jealousy to which the work renders one so vulnerable—including feelings of jealousy of that partially split off aspect of oneself which enjoys relatively close communion with the patient … the analyst is rendered lonely by his necessarily predominant attunement to aspects of the patient which are unconscious and which may not emerge into relatively full awareness for years … also transference can feel lonely that the patient is relating to an image of the analyst that has little basis at times in the analyst's own identity. (p. 135)

## Countertransference jealousy and the observing transference

There is a particular transference reaction that is especially prone to cause loneliness and jealousy in the analyst—the patient placing the analyst in the position of the excluded observer. This often occurs in the context of a patient being preoccupied with someone (or something) outside of the analytic setting that has no direct relationship with what is happening explicitly in the analytic process.

In these situations, the analyst often feels excluded and left to help-lessly observe the details of the patient's life with no real involvement—the transference is essentially one of the analyst being an observer to the patient's life (Steiner, 2011a). This can lead to unconscious jealous reactions in the analyst which can enact the need to include herself in order to avoid the pain of exclusion and the discomfort of jealousy.

Steiner (2011a) discusses this observing transference and the diffi-culty it poses to the analyst:

The observing transference is also difficult for the analyst to tolerate, and I have found that it is particularly conducive to enactments. This is especially the case when material is brought involving passionate feelings with no direct transference link—often, for example, when contentious incidents, say with a parent,

> a spouse or rival are reported. In these situations the analyst may
> try to force himself back into the primary role. (p. 87)

On an unconscious level, the analyst is reacting to losing the position of the patient's "primary object" and left to be an observer excluded from the action. This place of the excluded jealous observer is often unconscious and can lead to the analyst needing to force herself back into being on the inside by collapsing triadic reality. As Steiner (2011a) notes, one enactment that can occur is an overt attempt to include oneself by over-interpreting transference themes in the content of the patient's associations.

Although it is always important to understand the transference implications of all of the patient's associations, the jealous analyst may fall prey to actively imagining all of the patient's associations have some transference theme when in fact the important transference–countertransference theme is the cocreation of a feeling of exclusion and jealousy on the part of the analyst from the patient's inner world.

## Case example

In the chapter on Arrogance, I described my treatment with Molly, fifty-seven-year-old magazine editor and a mother of two boys, ages eighteen and sixteen, who began treatment with me after her analyst of fifteen years passed away. I want to focus here on my experience of feeling like an excluded observer in our treatment together, and the underlying jealous enactment that occurred between us.

Molly was significantly impaired in her ability to function due to severe anxiety and somatic symptoms including intermittent pains in her throat and neck with no clear medical cause. She spoke in a rapid and loud fashion staring straight ahead with only intermittent eye contact, with a flurry of complex ideas and verbiage that often caused me to feel confused and worried that I could not understand her. I began to also feel ashamed that I could not keep up with her complex ideas and thoughts that seemed to relentlessly take up the entire session. Most of her associations involved angry struggles with her ex-husband and her two sons, both of whom had developmental delays and behavioral issues. I found myself struggling to gain a foothold into her ideas and thoughts and wondered how often and when I could interrupt her to get a word in. Molly seemed to not want me to speak but she also was desperate to convey the urgency and severity of her situation and her symptoms to me.

Although at the time I did not realize it, my feelings of wanting to talk and interrupt her came from a feeling of jealousy over being excluded from her associations—they contained no meaningful bridge to our relationship or her present emotional state. I began to attempt to bring Molly into the "here and now" in our relationship together by commenting on how she might be feeling overwhelmed and frustrated in here with me as she did with her ex-husband. She agreed with this assessment but went on to talk about her situation in the same manner as before, effectively ignoring the comment. I began to feel left out and ignored, forced into the role of simply observing her associations without making any impact at all.

This was the role that Molly occupied in her family, being the fourth in a family of eight, born prematurely with a neurological disorder that affected her ability to walk. Molly grew up watching her brothers and sisters play together without her. Her mother was diagnosed with lupus and was often bedridden. When her mother was awake, she preferred the company of her eldest son, leaving Molly alone with her books. Over time, allowing myself to be more comfortable in the role of the observer and understanding its meaning to Molly let me be less jealous of her associations and allowed me to be more responsive and attuned to her suffering.

Molly's crushing jealousy experiences growing up forced her to use what Lewin (2011) describes as a defense of parallel identification, a manic defense that creates a non-penetrating state of relatedness in the transference that effectively blocks any ability for the analyst to reach the patient:

> The patient, anaesthetized to the conscious pain of jealousy, becomes emotionally frozen. This blocks the back-and-forth energy-flow of projective/introjective processes between patient and therapist, in turn distancing the therapist from the efficacy of internally articulating her countertransference. (p. 552)

Painfully bearing the position of the excluded observer can allow a place of empathy and respect for the patient's struggles which can lead to reduction in this defensive identification.

## Jealousy and seduction

Another method of the analyst avoiding conscious chronic jealousy is an enactment of various forms of seduction with the patient. Seduction can of course take on many forms in the analytic setting, ranging from verbal enactments to sexual acting out on the part of the analyst. This is a very obvious yet overlooked defense against the awareness of jealous feelings—a seduction collapses the triadic space and the pain of exclusion by creating a magical atmosphere of there being only two with no rivals or observers.

Several authors have discussed the seductive nature of the analytic setting in its exclusive focus on the relationship between the analyst and the analysand and how this is a necessary condition for the emergence of transference and a deepening of the analytic process (Maroda, 1998). In these conditions the analyst and patient are both vulnerable to jealous reactions when a third is introduced: "The discovery of the oedipal triangle is felt to be the death of the couple ... in this phantasy the arrival of the notion of the third always murders the dyadic relationship" (Britton, 1998, p. 37).

One form a seduction can take is to avoid triadic themes of jealousy, competitiveness, and sexuality by focusing on pre-oedipal conflicts involving separation and attachment to a maternal figure. In their discussion of a girl's developmental move from an exclusive relationship with the mother to a triadic sexual competitive relationship involving the father, Kulish and Holtzman (2008) describe how the analyst can impede a woman's progress towards a triadic experience with the father because of jealousy.

When jealous and competitive feelings begin to emerge in the transference between female analysts and their female patients, a female analyst may resist being seen as the rival mother—instead the analyst can move the analysis back to mother/daughter issues and focus on conflicts surrounding safety and attachment, ignoring the competitive strivings of the patient:

> Some female analysts respond defensively to the competition and envy of their female patients and often resist being seen as the rival triadic mother. Instead, they tend to get involved—or lost— in earlier "pre-Oedipal" mother/daughter issues, or to become identified with their patients. They may become "too maternal" and overprotective. (Kulish & Holtzman, 2008, p. 166)

This maternal "overprotectiveness" shields the analyst from her own jealous reactions to her patient's competitive wishes to take on the father as the love object and seductively eliminates the rival in the oedipal triangle.

In a similar manner male analysts, in an effort to avoid their own possessive and jealous feelings, may infantilize their female patients by taking on an overly paternal transference to avoid themes involving jealousy and sexuality, unconsciously seducing their patients into a magical union between the two with no rivals (Kulish & Holtzman, 2008).

In these cases, one finds an emphasis on a split between the idealized all loving "good" mother and the devalued cruel "bad mother." The analyst inhabits the role of the good parent, loving and caring for the patient who has been damaged and hurt. This seductively protects the couple from any intrusions from the "bad parent" who is split off and displaced onto a person outside the therapeutic situation—usually a spouse or an actual parental figure (Kulish & Holtzman, 2008). In effect, the analyst communicates to the patient, "Your parents were cruel and hurt you. I will be the loving parent you never had and not hurt or abandon you—no one will come between us." As Maroda (1998) notes:

> If I, the analyst, am not the bad object, and the patient needs to experience "someone" in that role, who else is left? ... That is why the safest possible situation for both patient and therapist is simply to stay outside the transference–countertransference interplay and let the real parents, spouse, boss, colleagues, etc. be the bad objects. (p. 23)

This phenomenon is common in case discussions where colleagues often vent their frustrations about the patient's parents and the harm they did. Although it is often the case that parents do significant harm to their children, the moral outrage and aggression towards the patient's parental figures may be ways of coping with unconscious jealous possessiveness towards their patients and the need to be the good object to preserve a dyadic union.

## Jealousy and the lovesick analyst

These themes of seduction and possessiveness of the patient are overtly seen in boundary violations between analyst and patient. Sexual boundary violations often begin with a lonely, "lovesick" analyst feeling the need to have the exclusive love of a patient she views as special (Gabbard & Lester, 1995). The lovesick analyst harbors an unconscious or conscious fantasy that love is healing, and that a psychic cure will occur if they love their patients more completely than their parents did—a common fantasy of patients entering analysis as well. This "love cure" is threatened by the emergence of conscious feelings of jealousy which interrupts the fantasy of the union between the two lovers. The analyst, lonely and jealous, needs to possess the patient fully in order to eliminate any jealous feelings—she must know that the patient is fully hers without any rival. A magical seductive space is created to harbor this illusion and perpetuate the fantasy of magical union.

Summing up, avoiding the unbearable "inside out" experience of jealousy by enclosing oneself in an imagined complete union with another is what this chapter is aiming to put into words. Somewhat surprisingly, the setup of the analytic relationship renders us vulnerable to jealousy because of our struggle of being intimately involved with our patients as well as being deprived of receiving the same nurturance in return. Despite this, our jealous countertransferences also offer opportunities for analytic growth—emerging conscious experiences of jealousy in both the patient and analyst can lead to a deeper appreciation of the patient's own struggles with jealousy and exclusion, allowing them to face the loss of the bliss of the primal union we all long to go back to.

# References

Abbasi, A. (2014). *The Rupture of Serenity: External Intrusions and Psychoanalytic Technique*. New York: Routledge.

Abbasi, A. (2015). The analyst's greed. In: S. Akhtar (Ed.), *Greed: Developmental, Cultural, and Clinical Realms* (pp. 207–224). London: Karnac.

Abbasi, A. (2018). The analyst's bodily sensations as important information in clinical work. *Psychoanalytic Inquiry, 38*: 530–540.

Abelove, H. (2016). Freud, male homosexuality, and the Americans revisited: A brief contribution to the history of psychoanalysis. *Studies in Gender and Sexuality, 17*: 78–79.

Adelman, A. (2016). The analyst's sense of shame. In: S. Akhtar (Ed.), *Shame: Developmental, Cultural and Clinical Realms* (pp. 184–204). New York: Routledge.

Akhtar, S. (1996). "Someday … " and "If only … " fantasies: Pathological optimism and inordinate nostalgia as related forms of idealization. *Journal of the American Psychoanalytic Association, 44*: 723–753.

Akhtar, S. (2003). Things: Developmental, psychopathological, and technical aspects of inanimate objects. *Canadian Journal of Psychoanalysis, 11*: 1–44.

Akhtar, S. (2007). From unmentalized xenophobia to messianic sadism: Some reflections on the phenomenology of prejudice. In: H. Parens, A. Mahfouz, S. Twemlow, and D. Scharff (Eds.), *The Future of Prejudice* (pp. 7–20). Lanham, MD: Jason Aronson.

Akhtar, S. (2009). *Comprehensive Dictionary of Psychoanalysis*. London: Karnac.

Akhtar, S. (2013). Guilt: An introductory overview. In: S. Akhtar (Ed.), *Guilt: Origins, Manifestations, and Management* (pp. 1–14). Lanham, MD: Jason Aronson.

Akhtar, S. (2015). Meanings, manifestations, and management of greed. In: S. Akhtar (Ed.), *Greed: Developmental, Cultural, and Clinical Realms* (pp. 131–158). London: Karnac.

Akhtar, S. (2018a). *Unusual Interventions: Alterations of the Frame, Method, and Relationship in Psychotherapy and Psychoanalysis*. New York: Routledge.

Akhtar, S. (2018b). *Sources of Suffering: Fear, Greed, Guilt, Deception, Betrayal, and Revenge*. New York: Routledge.

Akhtar, S. (2018c). *A Web of Sorrow: Mistrust, Jealousy, Lovelessness, Shamelessness, Regret, and Hopelessness*. New York: Routledge.

Allphin, C. (1982). Envy in the transference and countertransference. *Clinical Social Work Journal, 10*: 151–164.

Amati-Mehler, J., & Argentieri, S. (1989). Hope and hopelessness: A technical problem. *International Journal of Psychoanalysis, 70*: 295–304.

Aron, L. (1996). *A Meeting of Minds: Mutuality in Psychoanalysis*. New York: Analytic Press.

Aron, L., & Starr, K. E. (2013). *A Psychotherapy for the People: Toward a Progressive Psychoanalysis*. New York: Routledge.

Atlas, G. (2015). *The Enigma of Desire: Sex, Longing, and Belonging in Psychoanalysis*. New York: Routledge.

Atwood, G. E., & Stolorow, R. D. (2001). *Faces in a Cloud: Intersubjectivity in Personality Theory*. Lanham, MD: Jason Aronson.

Auchincloss, E. L., & Samberg, E. (2012). *Psychoanalytic Terms and Concepts* (4th edn). New Haven, CT: Yale University Press.

Balint, M. (1968). *The Basic Fault: Therapeutic Aspects of Regression*. London: Tavistock.

Banaji, M. R., & Greenwald, A. G. (2013). *Blindspot: Hidden Biases of Good People*. New York: Bantam, 2016.

Barthes, R. (1977). *A Lover's Discourse: Fragments*. New York: Hill & Wang.

Bateman, A. W., & Fonagy, P. (2016). *Mentalization-based Treatment for Personality Disorders: A Practical Guide*. Oxford: Oxford University Press.

Bateson, G. (1955). A theory of play and fantasy: A report on theoretical aspects of the project for the study of the role of paradoxes of abstractions in communication. *American Psychiatric Association, Psychiatric Research Reports*, 2: 39–51.

Baumgart, H. (1990). *Jealousy: Experiences and Solutions*. Chicago, IL: University of Chicago Press.

Beckett, S. (1984). *Worstward Ho*. New York: Grove.

Benjamin, J. (2018). *Beyond Doer and Done to*. New York: Routledge.

Benjamin, J., & Atlas, G. (2015). The "too muchness" of excitement: sexuality in light of excess, attachment and affect regulation. *International Journal of Psychoanalysis, 96*: 39–63.

Benvenuto, S. (2016). *What Are Perversions? Sexuality, Ethics, Psychoanalysis*. London: Karnac.

Berger, B., & Newman, S. (2012). *Money Talks: in Therapy, Society, and Life*. New York: Routledge.

Bergstein, A. (2018). *Bion and Meltzer's Expeditions into Unmapped Mental Life*. New York: Routledge.

Bion, W. R. (1958). On arrogance. *International Journal of Psychoanalysis, 39*: 144–146.

Bion, W. R. (1959). Attacks on linking. *International Journal of Psychoanalysis, 40*: 308–315.

Bion, W. R. (1962a). *Learning from Experience*. New York: Routledge.

Bion, W. R. (1962b). The psycho-analytic study of thinking. *International Journal of Psychoanalysis, 43*: 306–310.

Bion, W. R. (1963). *Elements of Psycho-Analysis*. New York: Routledge.

Bion, W. R. (1970). *Attention and Interpretation*. London: Tavistock.

Bion, W. R. (2005). *The Tavistock Seminars*. New York: Routledge.

Blake, W. (1988). Proverbs of hell. In: D. V. Erdman (Ed.), *The Complete Poetry and Prose of William Blake* (revised edn.). New York: Anchor.

Blechner, M. J. (2017). Dissociation among psychoanalysts about sexual boundary violations. In: J. Petrucelli & S. Schoen (Eds.), *Unknowable, Unspeakable, and Unsprung: Psychoanalytic Perspectives on Truth, Scandal, Secrets and Lies* (pp. 171–180). New York: Routledge.

Blevis, M. (2006). *Jealousy*. New York: Other Press.

Bloom, S. (1997). *Creating Sanctuary: Toward the Evolution of Sane Societies*. New York: Routledge.

Blos, P. (1965). *On Adolescence: A Psychoanalytic Interpretation*. New York: Free Press.

Blum, H. (1973). The concept of erotized transference. *Journal of the American Psychoanalytic Association, 21*: 61–76.

Blum, H. (2013). Dissociation and its disorders. *Psychoanalytic Inquiry, 33*: 427–438.

Bodnar, S. (2004). Remember where you come from: Dissociative process in multicultural individuals. *Psychoanalytic Dialogues, 14*: 581–603.

Bollas, C. (1983). Expressive uses of the countertransference—notes to the patient from oneself. *Contemporary Psychoanalysis, 19*: 1–33.

Bollas, C. (1987). *The Shadow of the Object: Psychoanalysis of Unthought Known*. London: Free Association.

Bolognini, S. (2004). *Psychoanalytic Empathy*. London: Free Association.

Borgogno, F. (2014). "Coming from afar" and "Temporarily becoming the patient without knowing it": Two necessary analytic conditions according to Ferenczi's later thought. *American Journal of Psychoanalysis, 74*: 302–312.

Boris, H. N. (1976). On hope: Its nature and psychotherapy. *International Review of Psycho-Analysis, 3*: 139–150.

Bornstein, M. (2020). "On and off the couch." IPA podcast, episode 58. http://ipaoffthecouch.org/2020/07/04/episode-58-to-make-a-meaningful-life-reflections-on-a-life-in-psychoanalysis-with-melvin-bornstein-md (last accessed March 17, 2022).

Botella, C., & Botella, S. (2005). *The Work of Psychic Figurability*. London: Routledge.

Boulanger, G. (2018). When is vicarious trauma a necessary therapeutic tool? *Psychoanalytic Psychology, 35*: 60–69.

Brenner, C. (1957). *An Elementary Textbook of Psychoanalysis*. New York: Random House, 1974.

Brenner, I. (2004). *Psychic Trauma: Dynamics, Symptoms and Treatment*. Lanham, MD: Jason Aronson.

Brenner, I. (2009). A new view from the Acropolis: Dissociative identity disorder. *Psychoanalytic Quarterly, 78*: 57–105.

Britton, R. (1998). *Belief and Imagination: Explorations in Psychoanalysis*. New York: Routledge.

Britton, R. (1999). Getting in on the act: The hysterical solution. *International Journal of Psychoanalysis, 80*: 1–14.

Britton, R. (2003). *Sex, Death, and the Superego: Experiences in Psychoanalysis.* London: Karnac.

Britton, R., & Steiner, J. (1994). Interpretation: Selected fact or overvalued idea? *International Journal of Psychoanalysis, 75*: 1069–1078.

Bromberg, P. M. (1991). On knowing one's patient inside out: The aesthetics of unconscious communication. *Psychoanalytic Dialogues, 1*(4): 399–422.

Bromberg, P. M. (1996). Standing in the spaces: The multiplicity of self and the psychoanalytic relationship. *Contemporary Psychoanalysis, 32*(4): 509–536.

Bromberg, P. M. (2003). Something wicked this way comes: Trauma, dissociation, and conflict: The space where psychoanalysis, cognitive science, and neuroscience overlap. *Psychoanalytic Psychology, 20*: 558–574.

Bromberg, P. M. (2008). Shrinking the tsunami: Affect regulation, dissociation, and the shadow of the flood. *Contemporary Psychoanalysis, 44*: 329–350.

Bromberg, P. M. (2012). *The Shadow of the Tsunami and the Growth of the Relational Mind.* New York: Routledge.

Broucek, F. J. (1991). *Shame and the Self.* New York: Guilford.

Brown, B. (2012). *Listening to Shame.* YouTube. https://youtube.com/watch?v=psN1DORYYV0 (last accessed March 17, 2022).

Brown, L. (2019). *Transformational Processes in Clinical Psychoanalysis.* New York: Routledge.

Busch, F. (2019). *The Analyst's Reveries: Explorations in Bion's Enigmatic Concept.* New York: Routledge.

Busch, F., Milrod, B., Aronson, A., & Singer, M. (2012). *Manual of Panic Focused Psychodynamic Psychotherapy—Extended Range.* New York: Routledge.

Busch, F., Milrod, B., Chen, C., & Singer, M. (2021). *Trauma Focused Psychodynamic Psychotherapy: A Step-by-Step Treatment Manual.* Oxford: Oxford University Press.

Carveth, D. (2006). Self-punishment as guilt evasion: Theoretical issues. *Canadian Journal of Psychoanalysis, 14*: 176–198.

Carveth, D. (2017). "Bion 3." YouTube. August 27, 2017. https://youtube.com/watch?v=2SDZuyysE0Q (last accessed March 17, 2022).

Casement, P. (1985). *Learning from the Patient.* New York: Guilford.

Casement, P. (2002). *Learning from Our Mistakes: Beyond Dogma in Psychoanalysis and Psychotherapy.* New York: Guilford.

Cavelzani, A., & Tronick, E. (2016). Dyadically expanded states of consciousness and therapeutic change in the interaction between analyst and adult patient. *Psychoanalytic Dialogues, 26*: 599–615.

Celenza, A. (2007). *Sexual Boundary Violations: Therapeutic, Supervisory, and Academic Contexts.* Lanham, MD: Jason Aronson.

Celenza, A. (2014). *Erotic Revelations: Clinical Applications and Perverse Scenarios.* London: Routledge.

Celenza, A., & Gabbard, G. O. (2003). Analysts who commit sexual boundary violations: A lost cause? *Journal of the American Psychoanalytic Association, 51*: 617–636.

Chaplan, R. (2013). How to help get stuck analyses unstuck. *Journal of the American Psychoanalytic Association, 61*: 591–604.

Chefetz, R. A. (2009). Waking the dead therapist. *Psychoanalytic Dialogues, 19*(4): 393–404.

Chefetz, R. A. (2015). *Intensive Psychotherapy for Persistent Dissociative Processes: The Fear of Feeling Real.* New York: W. W. Norton.

Clarkin, J., Yeomans, F., & Kernberg O. F. (1998). *Psychotherapy for Borderline Personality.* Hoboken, NJ: John Wiley & Sons.

Coen, S. J. (1987). Pathological jealousy. *International Journal of Psychoanalysis, 68*: 99–108.

Coen, S. J. (2002). *Affect Intolerance in Patient and Analyst.* Lanham, MD: Jason Aronson.

Coen, S. J. (2003). The thrall of the negative and how to analyze it. *Journal of the American Psychoanalytic Association, 51*: 465–489.

Coen, S. J. (2013). Guilt in the therapist and its impact upon treatment. In: S. Akhtar (Ed.), *Guilt: Origins, Manifestations, and Management* (pp. 69–82). Lanham, MD: Jason Aronson.

Coltart, N. (1993). *How to Survive as a Psychotherapist.* Bicester, UK: Phoenix, 2020.

Cooper, S. H. (2011). *A Disturbance in the Field: Essays in Transference-Countertransference Engagement.* New York: Routledge.

Cooper, S. H. (2016). *The Analyst's Experience of the Depressive Position: The Melancholic Errand of Psychoanalysis.* New York: Routledge.

Courtois, C. A. (1988). *Healing the Incest Wound.* New York: W. W. Norton.

Crastnopol, M. (2015). *Micro-trauma.* New York: Routledge.

Dalenberg, C. (2000). *Countertransference and the Treatment of Trauma.* Washington, DC: American Psychological Association.

Danielian, J., & Gianotti, P. (2012). *Listening with Purpose: Entry Points into Shame and Narcissistic Vulnerability.* Lanham, MD: Jason Aronson.

Danto, E. (2005). *Freud's Free Clinics: Psychoanalysis and Social Justice.* New York: Columbia University Press.

Davids, F. (2011). *Internal Racism: A Psychoanalytic Approach to Race.* London: Red Globe.

Davies, J. M. (1994). Love in the afternoon: A relational consideration of desire and dread in the countertransference. *Psychoanalytic Dialogues, 4*: 153–170.

Davies, J. M. (2013). My enfant terrible is twenty: A discussion of Slavin's and Gentile's retrospective reconsideration of "Love in the Afternoon". *Psychoanalytic Dialogues, 23*: 170–179.

Davies, J. M., & Frawley, M. G. (1994). *Treating the Adult Survivor of Childhood Sexual Abuse: A Psychoanalytic Perspective.* New York: Basic Books.

Dean, T., & Lane, C. (2001). Homosexuality and psychoanalysis: An introduction. In: T. Dean & C. Lane (Eds.), *Homosexuality and Psychoanalysis* (pp. 3–43). Chicago, IL: University of Chicago Press.

DeYoung, P. (2015). *Understanding and Treating Chronic Shame: A Relational/Neurobiological Approach.* New York: Routledge.

Diamond, D., Yeomans, F. E., Stern, B. L., & Kernberg, O. F. (2021). *Treating Pathological Narcissism with Transference-Focused Psychotherapy.* New York: Guilford.

Diamond, M. J. (2020). Return of the repressed: Revisiting dissociation and the psychoanalysis of the traumatized mind. *Journal of the American Psychoanalytic Association, 68*: 839–874.

Dimen, M. (2011). *With Culture in Mind.* New York: Routledge.

Ellis, H. (1922). *Little Essays of Love and Virtue.* London: Read.

Eng, D., & Han, S. (2019). *Racial Melancholia, Racial Dissociation: On the Social and Psychic Lives of Asian Americans.* Durham, NC: Duke University Press.

Epstein, M. (2018). *Advice Not Given: A Guide to Getting over Yourself.* New York: Penguin.

Eshel, O. (2019). *The Emergence of Analytic Oneness: Into the Heart of Psychoanalysis.* New York: Routledge.

Faimberg, H. (2001). *The Telescoping of Generations.* London: Routledge.

Faimberg, H. (2013). "Well, you'd better ask them": The countertransference position at the crossroads. In: R. Oelsner (Ed.), *Transference and Countertransference Today* (pp. 49–66). New York: Routledge.

Fanon, F. (1952). *Black Skin, White Masks.* New York: Grove.

Fanon, F. (1961). *The Wretched of the Earth*. New York: Grove.

Farber, H. (1958). The therapeutic despair. *Psychiatry, 21*(1): 7–20.

Feldman, M. (2009). *Doubt, Conviction and the Analytic Process: Selected Papers of Michael Feldman*. New York: Routledge.

Fenichel, O. (1945). *The Psychoanalytic Theory of Neurosis*. New York: W. W. Norton.

Ferro, A. (2002). *In the Analyst's Consulting Room*. New York: Routledge.

Ferenczi, S. (1928). On the technique of psychoanalysis. In: S. Ferenczi (Ed.), *Further Contributions to the Theory and Technique of Psychoanalysis*. London: Karnac, 1980.

Figley, C. (1995). *Compassion Fatigue: Coping with Secondary Traumatic Stress Disorder in Those Who Treat the Traumatized*. New York: Routledge.

Fink, B. (2007). *The Fundamentals of Analytic Technique: A Lacanian Approach for Practitioners*. New York: W. W. Norton.

Finkelhor, D. (2019). Childhood sexual abuse: Challenges facing child protection and mental health professionals. In: E. Ullmann & W. Hilweg (Eds.), *Childhood and Trauma: Separation, Abuse, War* (pp. 101–116). New York: Routledge.

Finkelhor, D., Shattuck, A., Turner, H., & Hamby, S. (2014). The lifetime prevalence of child sexual abuse and sexual assault assessed in late adolescence. *Journal of Adolescent Health, 55*(3): 329–333.

Fonagy, P., & Higgitt, A. (2007). The development of prejudice: An attachment theory hypothesis explaining its ubiquity. In: H. Parens, A. Mahfouz, S. W. Twemlow, & D. E. Scharff (Eds.), *The Future of Prejudice: Psychoanalysis and the Prevention of Prejudice* (pp. 63–80). Lanham, MD: Jason Aronson.

Fors, M. (2018). *A Grammar of Power in Psychotherapy: Exploring the Dynamics of Privilege*. Washington, DC: American Psychological Association Press.

Freedenthal, S. (2018). *Helping the Suicidal Person: Tips and Techniques for Professionals*. New York: Routledge.

Freud, S. (1883). Letter from Sigmund Freud to Martha Bernays, September 16, 1883. In: E. L. Freud (Ed.), *Letters of Sigmund Freud, 1873–1939* (pp. 58–66). London: Hogarth, 1960.

Freud, S., & Breuer, J. (1895d). *Studies on Hysteria. S. E., 2*. London: Hogarth.

Freud, S. (1905d). *Three Essays on the Theory of Sexuality. S. E., 7*: 123–246. London: Hogarth.

Freud, S. (1909). Letter from Sigmund Freud to C. G. Jung, June 7, 1909. In: *The Freud/Jung Letters: The Correspondence between Sigmund Freud and C. G. Jung*, 41 (pp. 230–232). Princeton, NJ: Princeton University Press, 1974.

Freud, S. (1910d). The future prospects of psycho-analytic therapy. *S. E.*, *11*: 139–152. London: Hogarth.

Freud, S. (1912e). Recommendations to physicians practising psycho-analysis. *S. E.*, *12*: 109–120. London: Hogarth.

Freud, S. (1914g). Remembering, repeating and working-through (further recommendations on the technique of psycho-analysis, II). *S. E.*, *12*: 145–156. London: Hogarth.

Freud, S. (1915a). Observations on transference-love (further recommendations on the technique of psycho-analysis), III. *S. E.*, *12*: 157–171. London: Hogarth.

Freud, S. (1918b). From the history of an infantile neurosis. *S. E.*, *17*: 1–122. London: Hogarth.

Freud, S. (1919h). The "uncanny". *S. E.*, *17*: 217–256. London: Hogarth.

Freud, S. (1922b). Some neurotic mechanisms in jealousy, paranoia and homosexuality. *S. E.*, *18*: 221–232. London: Hogarth.

Freud, S. (1923b). *The Ego and the Id. S. E.*, *19*: 6–63. London: Hogarth.

Freud, S. (1936a). A disturbance of memory on the Acropolis. *S. E.*, *22*: 237–248. London: Hogarth.

Freud, S. (1937c). Analysis terminable and interminable. *S. E.*, *23*: 211–253. London: Hogarth.

Gabbard, G. O. (1996). *Love and Hate in the Analytic Setting*. Lanham, MD: Jason Aronson.

Gabbard, G. O. (2014). *Psychodynamic Psychiatry in Clinical Practice: 5th Edition*. Arlington, VA: American Psychiatric Publishing.

Gabbard, G. O. (2017). Sexual boundary violations in psychoanalysis: A 30-year retrospective. *Psychoanalytic Psychology*, 34(2): 151–156.

Gabbard, G. O., & Lester, E. P. (1995). *Boundaries and Boundary Violations in Psychoanalysis*. Washington, DC: American Psychiatric Publishing.

Garrett, M. (2019). *Psychotherapy for Psychosis. Integrating Cognitive-Behavioral and Psychodynamic Treatment*. New York: Guilford.

Gartner, R. B. (2014). Trauma and countertrauma, resilience and counterresilience. *Contemporary Psychoanalysis*, *50*: 609–626.

Gaztambide, D. (2019). *A People's History of Psychoanalysis*. Lanham, MD: Lexington.

George, S. (2016). *Trauma and Race: A Lacanian Study of African American Racial Identity*. Waco, TX: Baylor University Press.

George, S., & Hook, D. (2021). Theorizing race, racism, and racial identification. In: S. George & D. Hook (Eds.), *Racism, Identity and Psychoanalytic Theory* (pp. 15–28). New York: Routledge.

Ghent, E. (1990). Masochism, submission, surrender: Masochism as a perversion of surrender. *Contemporary Psychoanalysis, 26*: 108–136.

Gherovici, P. (2021). The lost souls of the barrio: Lacanian psychoanalysis in the ghetto. In: S. George & D. Hook (Eds.), *Racism, Identity and Psychoanalytic Theory* (pp. 189–209). New York: Routledge.

Gilhooley, D. (2002). Misrepresentation and misreading in the case of Anna O. *Modern Psychoanalysis, 27*: 75–100.

Giovacchini, P. (1993). *Countertransference Triumphs and Catastrophes.* Lanham, MD: Jason Aronson.

Goldberg, A. (2012). *The Analysis of Failure: An Investigation of Failed Cases in Psychoanalysis and Psychotherapy.* New York: Routledge.

Goldberg, P. (2020). Body-mind dissociation, altered states, and alter worlds. *Journal of the American Psychoanalytic Association, 68*: 769–806.

Grinberg, L. (1962). On a specific aspect of countertransference due to the patient's projective identification. *International Journal of Psychoanalysis, 43*: 436–440.

Grosskurth, P. (1991). *The Secret Ring: Freud's Inner Circle and the Politics of Psychoanalysis.* Boston, MA: Da Capo.

Grubrich-Simitis, I. (1997). *Early Freud and Late Freud.* London: Routledge.

Hainer, M. (2016). The Ferenczi paradox: His importance in understanding dissociation and the dissociation of his importance in psychoanalysis. In: E. Howell, E. Itzkowitz, & S. Itzkowitz (Eds.), *The Dissociative Mind in Psychoanalysis: Understanding and Working With Trauma* (pp. 57–70). New York: Routledge.

Hamer, F. (2012). Anti-racism and conceptions of whiteness. In: S. Akhtar (Ed.), *The African American Experience* (pp. 217–229). Lanham, MD: Rowman & Littlefield.

Hart, S. L., Carrington, H. A., Tronick, E. Z., & Carroll, S. R. (2004). When infants lose exclusive maternal attention: Is it jealousy? *Infancy, 6*: 57–78.

Heimann, P. (1950). On counter-transference. *International Journal of Psychoanalysis, 31*: 81–84.

Herman, J. (1992). *Trauma and Recovery: The Aftermath of Violence from Domestic Abuse to Political Terror.* New York: Basic Books.

Herman, J. (2012). Shattered shame states and their repair. In: J. Yellin & K. White (Eds.), *Shattered States: Disorganized Attachment and Its Repair* (pp. 157–170). London: Karnac.

Hinshelwood, R. D. (2013). Freud's countertransference? Reviewing the case histories with modern ideas of transference and countertransference. In: R. Oelsner (Ed.), *Transference and Countertransference Today* (pp. 88–105). New York: Routledge.

Hirsch, I. (1993). Countertransference enactments and some issues related to external factors in the analyst's life. *Psychoanalytic Dialogues, 3*: 343–366.

Hirsch, I. (2008). *Coasting in the Countertransference: Conflicts of Self Interest between Analyst and Patient.* New York: Analytic Press.

Hirsch, I. (2014). Narcissism, mania, and analysts' envy of patients. *Psychoanalytic Inquiry, 34*: 408–420.

Holmes, D. (1999). Race and countertransference: Two "blind spots" in psychoanalytic perception. *Journal of Applied Psychoanalytic Studies, 1*(4): 319–333.

Hook, D. (2018). *Six Moments in Lacan: Communication and Identification in Psychology and Psychoanalysis.* New York: Routledge.

Hook, D. (2021). Pilfered pleasure: On racism as "the theft of enjoyment." In: S. George & D. Hook (Eds.), *Racism, Identity and Psychoanalytic Theory* (pp. 35–50). New York: Routledge.

hooks, b. (1995). *Killing Rage: Ending Racism.* New York: Henry Holt.

Hopenwasser, K. (2008). Being in rhythm: Dissociative attunement in therapeutic process. *Journal of Trauma and Dissociation, 9*(3): 349–367.

Howell, E. (2005). *The Dissociative Mind.* New York: Routledge.

Howell, E. (2020). *Trauma and Dissociation Informed Psychotherapy: Relational Healing and the Therapeutic Connection.* New York: W. W. Norton.

Jacquet, J. (2015). *Is Shame Necessary? Uses for an Old Tool.* New York: Vintage.

Jones, E. (1929). Fear, guilt and hate. *International Journal of Psychoanalysis, 10*: 383–397.

Jurist, E. (2018). *Minding Emotions: Cultivating Mentalization in Psychotherapy.* New York: Guilford.

Kahr, B. (1996). *D. W. Winnicott: A Biographical Portrait.* New York: Routledge.

Kahr, B. (2020). *Bombs in the Consulting Room: Surviving Psychological Shrapnel.* New York: Routledge.

Kaplan, M. (1979). *The Jewish Feminist Movement in Germany: The Campaigns of the Judischer Frauenbund.* Westport, CT: Praeger.

Karpman, S. (1968). Fairy tales and script drama analysis. *Transactional Analysis Bulletin, 7*: 39–43.

Keats, J. (1817). Letter to George and Thomas Keats, 21 December 1817. In: J. P. Hunter (Ed.), *The Norton Introduction to Literature: Poetry*. New York: W. W. Norton, 1973.

Kernberg, O. F. (1994). Love in the analytic setting. *Journal of the American Psychoanalytic Association, 42*: 1137–1157.

Kernberg, O. F., & Michels, R. (2016). Thoughts on the present and future of psychoanalytic education. *Journal of the American Psychoanalytic Association, 64*: 385–407.

Keval, N. (2016). *Racist States of Mind*. London: Karnac.

Khan, M. M. R. (1972). Dread of surrender to resourceless dependence in the analytic situation. *International Journal of Psychoanalysis, 53*: 225–230.

Khan, M. M. R. (1974). Vicissitudes of being, knowing, and experiencing in the therapeutic situation. In: *The Privacy of the Self* (pp. 203–218). New York: International Universities Press.

Kilborne, B. (2002). *Disappearing Persons: Shame and Appearance*. Albany, NY: State University of New York Press.

Klein, M. (1935). A contribution to the psychogenesis of manic-depressive states. In: *Love, Guilt, and Reparation and Other Works 1921–1945* (pp. 262–289). New York: Free Press, 1992.

Klein, M. (1948). A contribution to the theory of anxiety and guilt. *International Journal of Psychoanalysis, 29*: 114–123.

Kluft, R. P. (1996). Dissociative identity disorder. In: L. K. Michelson & W. J. Ray (Eds.), *Handbook of Dissociation: Theoretical, Empirical, and Clinical Perspectives* (pp. 337–366). New York: Plenum.

Knafo, D., & Bosco, R. (2020). *The New Sexual Landscape and Contemporary Psychoanalysis*. London: Confer.

Knoblauch, S. H. (2020). *Bodies and Social Rhythms*. New York: Routledge.

Koch, E. (2000). Representations of dread: The dreaded self and the dreaded state of the self. *Psychoanalytic Quarterly, 69*: 289–316.

Kristeva, J. (1982). *Powers of Horror: An Essay on Abjection*. New York: Columbia University Press.

Kulish, N., & Holtzman, D. (2008). *A Story of Her Own: The Female Oedipus Complex Reexamined and Renamed*. Lanham, MD: Jason Aronson.

Kumin, I. (1985). Erotic horror: Desire and resistance in the psychoanalytic situation. *International Journal Psychoanalytic Psychotherapy, 11*: 3–20.

Lacan, J. (1973). *The Four Fundamental Concepts of Psychoanalysis: Book XI*. New York: W. W. Norton.

Ladany, N., Klinger, R., & Kulp, L. (2011). Therapist shame: Implications for therapy and supervision. In: R. L. Dearing and J. P. Tangey (Eds.), *Shame in the Therapy Hour* (pp. 307–322). Washington, DC: American Psychological Association.

Lansky, M. R. (2005). The impossibility of forgiveness: Shame fantasies as instigators of vengefulness in Euripides' Medea. *Journal of the American Psychoanalytic Association, 53*: 437–464.

Lansky, M. R. (2007). Unbearable shame, splitting, and forgiveness in the resolution of vengefulness. *Journal of the American Psychoanalytic Association, 55*: 571–593.

Lansky. M. R. (2016). Shame and the aversion to apologizing. In: S. Akhtar (Ed.), *Shame: Developmental, Cultural and Clinical Realms* (pp. 129–140). New York: Routledge.

Laplanche, J., & Pontalis, J. B. (1973). *The Language of Psycho-Analysis*. London: Hogarth.

Lear, J. (2003). Confidentiality as a virtue. In: C. Levin, C. A. Furlong, & M. K. O'Neil (Eds.), *Confidentiality: Ethical and Clinical Dilemmas* (pp. 3–18). New York: Routledge.

Lear, J. (2005). *Freud*. New York: Routledge.

Leary, K. (2000). Racial enactments in dynamic treatment. *Psychoanalytic Dialogues, 10*: 639–653.

Levin, S. (1967). Some metapsychological considerations on the differentiation between shame and guilt. *International Journal of Psychoanalysis, 48*(2): 267–276.

Lewin, S. (2011). Parallel identification: A shield against the assault of traumatic jealousy. *Psychoanalytic Dialogues, 21*: 551–570.

Lewis, H. B. (1971). *Shame and Guilt in Neurosis*. Madison, CT: International Universities Press.

Lewis, M. (1992). *Shame: The Exposed Self*. New York: Free Press.

Loewald, H. W. (1960). On the therapeutic action of psycho-analysis. *International Journal of Psychoanalysis, 41*: 16–33.

Loewald, H. W. (1986). Transference-countertransference. *Journal of the American Psychoanalytic Association, 34*: 275–287.

Lombardi, R. (2002). Primitive mental states and the body. *International Journal of Psychoanalysis, 83*: 363–381.

Lombardi, R. (2008). The body in the analytic session: Focusing on the body-mind link. *International Journal of Psychoanalysis, 89*: 89–110.

Lombardi, R. (2009). Through the eye of the needle: The unfolding of the unconscious body. *Journal of the American Psychoanalytic Association, 57*: 61–94.

Lombardi, R. (2017). *Body-Mind Dissociation in Psychoanalysis: Development after Bion.* New York: Routledge.

Lynd, H. M. (1958). *On Shame and the Search for Identity.* New York: Harcourt, Brace & World.

Makari, G. (2008). *Revolution in Mind: The Creation of Psychoanalysis.* New York: HarperCollins.

Maltsberger, J., & Buie, D. (1974). Countertransference hate in the treatment of suicidal patients. *Archives of General Psychiatry, 30*(5): 625–633.

Markman, H. C. (2020). Embodied attunement and participation. *Journal of the American Psychoanalytic Association, 68*: 807–834.

Maroda, K. (1998). *Seduction, Surrender and Transformation: Emotional Engagement in the Analytic Process.* New York: Analytic Press.

Mbembe, A. (2016). Frantz Fanon and the politics of viscerality. Keynote lecture. John Hope Franklin Humanities Institute, Duke University, Durham, NC. YouTube. https://youtube.com/watch?v=lg_BEodNaEA (last accessed March 17, 2022).

McCann, I. L., & Pearlman, L. A. (1990). Vicarious traumatization: A framework for understanding the psychological effects of working with victims. *Journal of Traumatic Stress, 3*: 131–150.

McGowan, T. (2021). The bedlam of the lynch mob: Racism and enjoying through the other. In: S. George & D. Hook (Eds.), *Racism, Identity and Psychoanalytic Theory* (pp. 31–45). New York: Routledge.

McGuire, W. (1974). *The Freud/Jung Letters.* London: Hogarth & Routledge.

McWilliams, N. (1996). Therapy across the sexual orientation boundary: Reflections of a heterosexual female analyst on working with lesbian, gay, and bisexual patients. *Gender and Psychoanalysis, 1*: 203–221.

McWilliams, N. (2004). *Psychoanalytic Therapy: A Practitioner's Guide.* New York: Guilford.

McWilliams, N. (2011). *Psychoanalytic Diagnosis* (2nd edn). New York: Guilford.

Menaker, E. (1989). *Appointment in Vienna: An American Psychoanalyst Recalls Her Student Days in Pre-War America.* New York: St. Martin's.

Menninger, K. (1958). *Theory of Psychoanalytic Technique.* New York: Basic Books.

Meszaros, J. (2015). Ferenczi in our contemporary world. In: A. Harris & S. Kuchuck (Eds.), *The Legacy of Sandor Ferenczi: From Ghost to Ancestor* (pp. 19–32). New York: Routledge.

Mitchell, J. (1974). *Psychoanalysis and Feminism*. London: Allen Lane.

Mitchell, S. (1993). *Hope and Dread in Psychoanalysis*. New York: Basic Books.

Mollon, P. (2018). *Shame and Jealousy: The Hidden Turmoils*. New York: Routledge.

Morrison, A. (1989). *Shame: The Underside of Narcissism*. London: Analytic Press.

Moskowitz, A., Heinimaa, M., & van der Hart, O. (2019). Defining psychosis, trauma and dissociation: Historical and contemporary conceptions. In: A. Moskowitz, M. Dorathy, & I. Schafer (Eds.), *Psychosis, Trauma and Dissociation: Evolving Perspectives on Severe Psychopathology* (pp. 9–31). Hoboken, NJ: John Wiley & Sons.

National Institute of Mental Health Website (2021). *Suicide Rates*. https://nimh. nih.gov/health/statistics/suicide (last accessed January 3, 2021).

Newirth, J. (2016). A Kleinian perspective on dissociation and trauma: Miscarriages in symbolization. In: E. Howell & S. Itzkowitz (Eds.), *The Dissociative Mind in Psychoanalysis: Understanding and Working with Trauma* (pp. 107–117). New York: Routledge.

Nietzsche, F. W. (1990). *Beyond Good and Evil: Prelude to a Philosophy of the Future*. New York: Penguin.

Nijenhuis, E., & Van der Hart, O. (2011). Dissociation in trauma: A new definition and comparison with previous formulations. *Journal of Trauma and Dissociation, 12*(4): 416–445.

Nunberg, H. (1955). *Principles of Psychoanalysis*. New York: International Universities Press.

Oelsner, R. (2013). Introduction. In: R. Oelsner (Ed.), *Transference and Countertransference Today* (pp. 1–17). New York: Routledge.

Ogden, T. H. (1997). Reverie and metaphor: Some thoughts on how I work as a psychoanalyst. *International Journal of Psychoanalysis, 78*: 719–732.

Oliver, M. (2015). *Dog Songs: Thirty-five Dog Songs and One Essay*. New York: Penguin.

Orgel, S. (2012). On negative therapeutic reaction. In: L. Wurmser & H. Jarass (Eds.), *Nothing Good Is Allowed to Stand: An Integrative View of the Negative Therapeutic Reaction* (pp. 57–66). New York: Routledge.

Panksepp, J. (1998). *Affective Neuroscience: The Foundations of Human and Animal Emotions.* New York: Oxford University Press.

Parsons, M. (2000). *The Dove that Returns, the Dove that Vanishes: Paradox and Creativity in Psychoanalysis.* London: Routledge.

Patraka, V. (1992). Binary terror and feminist performance: Reading both ways. *Discourse, 4*(2): 163–185.

Pearlman, L. A., & Saakvitne, K. W. (1995). *Trauma and the Therapist: Countertransference and Vicarious Traumatization in Psychotherapy with Incest Survivors.* New York: W. W. Norton.

Philips, A. (2019). The simplicity of shame. *Salmagundi Magazine,* Spring/Summer. https://salmagundi.skidmore.edu/articles/139-the-simplicity-of-shame (last accessed March 14, 2022).

Piers, G. (1953). Shame and guilt: A psychoanalytic study. In: G. Piers & M. Singer (Eds.), *Shame and Guilt* (pp. 15–55). New York: W. W. Norton.

Pinsky, E. (2017). *Death and Fallibility in the Psychoanalytic Encounter: Mortal Gifts.* New York: Routledge.

Plotkin, M. (2018). Freud and the Latin Americans: A forgotten relationship. In: P. Gherovici & C. Christian (Eds.), *Psychoanalysis in the Barrio: Race, Class and the Unconscious* (pp. 21–37). New York: Routledge.

Poland, W. S. (2013). The analyst's approach and the patient's psychic growth. *Psychoanalytic Quarterly, 82*: 829–847.

Poland, W. S. (2018). *Intimacy and Separateness in Psychoanalysis.* New York: Routledge.

Powell, D. (2012). Psychoanalysis and African Americans: Past, present and future. In: S. Akhtar (Ed.), *The African American Experience: Psychoanalytic Perspectives* (pp. 59–84). Lanham, MD: Jason Aronson.

Powell, D. (2018). Race, African Americans, and psychoanalysis: Collective silence in the therapeutic situation. *Journal of the American Psychoanalytic Association, 66*(6): 1021–1049.

Powell, D. (2021). Race matters in psychoanalytic education. *Psychoanalysis Today.* https://psychoanalysis.today/en-GB/PT-Articles/Powell139922/Race-Matters-in-Psychoanalytic-Education.aspx (last accessed March 17, 2022).

Purcell, S. D. (2020). Dissociation: Dissemblance or dis-assembly? Commentary on Diamond. *Journal of the American Psychoanalytic Association, 68*: 889–906.

Putnam, F. W. (1997). *Dissociation in Children and Adolescents: A Developmental Perspective.* New York: Guilford.

Rachman, A. (2018). *Elizabeth Severn: The "Evil Genius" of Psychoanalysis.* New York: Routledge.

Racker, H. (1957). The meanings and uses of countertransference. *Psychoanalytic Quarterly, 26*: 303–357.

Racker, H. (1968). *Transference and Counter-Transference.* Madison, CT: International Universities Press.

Reik, T. (1948). *Listening with the Third Ear: The Inner Experience of a Psychoanalyst.* New York: Farrar, Straus.

Reis, B. (2011). Zombie states: Reconsidering the relationship between life and death instincts. *Psychoanalytic Quarterly, 80*: 269–286.

Reis, B. (2020). *Creative Repetition and Intersubjectivity.* New York: Routledge.

Renik, O. (2006). *Practical Psychoanalysis for Therapists and Patients.* New York: Other Press.

Riviere, J. (1932). Jealousy as a mechanism of defense. *International Journal of Psychoanalysis, 13*: 414–424.

Ronson, J. (2015). *So You've Been Publicly Shamed.* New York: Penguin.

Rosenfeld, H. (1971). Contribution to the psychopathology of psychotic states; the importance of projective identification in the ego structure and the object relations of the psychotic patient. In: P. Doucet & C. Lauren (Eds.), *Problems of Psychosis* (pp. 115–128). The Hague: Excerpta Medica.

Sadek, N. (2020). The phenomenology and dynamics of wealth shame: Between moral responsibility and moral masochism. *Journal of the American Psychoanalytic Association, 68*: 615–648.

Safán-Gerard, D. (2013). Bearable and unbearable guilt: A Kleinian perspective. In: S. Akhtar (Ed.), *Guilt: Origins, Manifestations, and Management* (pp. 41–58). Lanham, MD: Jason Aronson.

Safán-Gerard, D. (2019). Victims of envy. *Psychoanalytic Review, 106*(3): 225–245.

Safran, J., & Muran, C. (2000). *Negotiating the Therapeutic Alliance: A Relational Treatment Guide.* New York: Guilford.

Schechter, M., Ronningstam, E., Herbstman, B., & Goldblatt, M. J. (2019). Psychotherapy with suicidal patients: The integrative psychodynamic approach of the Boston Suicide Study Group. *Medicina, 55*(6): 303.

Scheff, T. J. (1987). The shame rage spiral: A case study of an interminable quarrel. In: H. B. Lewis (Ed.), *The Role of Shame in Symptom Formation* (pp. 109–150). Hillsdale, NJ: Lawrence Erlbaum.

Schmithusen, G. (2012). "Time that no one can count, always begins anew": Thoughts concerning the function and meaning of the so-called negative therapeutic reaction from the perspective of time standing still. In: L. Wurmser & H. Jarass (Eds.), *Nothing Good Is Allowed to Stand: An Integrative View of the Negative Therapeutic Reaction* (pp. 67–96). New York: Routledge.

Schneidman, E. (1993). *Suicide as Psychache*. Lanham, MD: Jason Aronson.

Schore, A. N. (2003). *Affect Regulation and the Repair of the Self*. New York: W. W. Norton.

Schore, A. N. (2009). Attachment trauma and the developing right brain: Origins of pathological dissociation. In: P. F. & J. F. O'Neil (Eds.), *Dissociation and the Dissociative Disorders: DSM V and Beyond* (pp. 107–141). New York: Routledge.

Schore, A. N. (2019). *The Development of the Unconscious Mind*. New York: W. W. Norton.

Schwaber, E. A. (2005). The struggle to listen: Continuing reflections, lingering paradoxes, and some thoughts on the recovery of memory. *Journal of the American Psychoanalytic Association, 53*: 789–810.

Schwartz, H. J., & Ceaser, M. (2005). The patient with bulimia. In: H. J. Schwartz, E. Bleiberg, & S. H. Weissman (Eds.), *Psychodynamic Concepts in General Psychiatry* (pp. 335–357). Washington, DC: American Psychiatric Press.

Searles, H. (1979). *Countertransference and Related Subjects*. New York: International Universities Press.

Searles, H. (1986). *My Work with Borderline Patients*. London: Jason Aronson.

Sedgwick, E., & Frank, A. (Eds.) (1995). *Shame and Its Sisters: A Silvan Tomkins Reader*. Durham, NC: Duke University Press.

Sedlak, V. (2019). *The Psychoanalyst's Superegos, Ego Ideals and Blind Spots*. New York: Routledge.

Shah, D. (in press). When racialized ghosts refuse to become ancestors: Tasting Loewald's "blood of recognition" in racial melancholia and mixed-race identities. *Psychoanalytic Dialogues*.

Shapiro, S. A. (1993). Gender-role stereotypes and clinical process: Commentary on papers by Gruenthal and Hirsch. *Psychoanalytic Dialogues, 3*: 371–387.

Shamay-Tsoory, S. (2011). Empathic processing: Its cognitive and affective dimensions and neuroanatomical basis. In: J. Decety & W. Ickes (Eds.), *The Social Neuroscience of Empathy* (pp. 215–232). Cambridge, MA: Massachusetts Institute of Technology Press.

Shea, S. C. (2011). *The Practical Art of Suicide Assessment: A Guide for Mental Health Professionals and Substance Abuse Counselors*. Hoboken, NJ: John Wiley & Sons.

Shedler, J. (2010). The efficacy of psychodynamic psychotherapy. *American Psychologist, 65*(2): 98–109.

Shorter, E. (1997). *A History of Psychiatry: From the Era of the Asylum to the Age of Prozac.* New York: John Wiley & Sons.

Sletvold, J. (2014). *The Embodied Analyst: From Freud and Reich to Relationality.* New York: Routledge.

Slochower, J. (2006). *Psychoanalytic Collisions.* London: Analytic Press.

Solms, M. (2018). The neurobiological underpinnings of psychoanalytic theory and therapy. *Frontiers in Behavioral Neuroscience, 12*: 294.

Spezzano, C. (2007). A home for the mind. *Psychoanalytic Quarterly, 765*(supplement): 1563–1583.

Spillius, E. B., Milton, J., Garvey, P., Couve, C., & Steiner, D. (2011). *The New Dictionary of Kleinian Thought.* New York: Routledge.

Stein, R. (1997). The shame experiences of the analyst. *Progress in Self Psychology, 13*: 109–123.

Stein, R. (2008). The otherness of sexuality: Excess. *Journal of the American Psychoanalytic Association, 56*: 43–71.

Steiner, J. (1993). *Psychic Retreats: Pathological Organizations in Psychotic, Neurotic and Borderline Patients.* New York: Routledge.

Steiner, J. (2011a). *Seeing and Being Seen: Emerging from a Psychic Retreat.* New York: Routledge.

Steiner, J. (2011b). Helplessness and the exercise of power in the analytic session. *International Journal of Psychoanalysis, 92*(1): 135–147.

Steiner, J. (2015). Seeing and being seen: Shame in the clinical situation. *International Journal of Psychoanalysis, 96*: 1589–1601.

Stephens, M. A. (2014). *Skin Acts: Race, Psychoanalysis and the Black Male Performer.* Durham, NC: Duke University Press.

Stern, D. B. (2004). The eye sees itself: Dissociation, enactment, and the achievement of conflict. *Contemporary Psychoanalysis, 40*: 197–237.

Stern, D. B. (2009). *Partners in Thought: Working with Unformulated Experience, Dissociation, and Enactment.* New York: Routledge.

Stern, D. B. (2015). *Relational Freedom: Emergent Properties of the Interpersonal Field.* New York: Routledge.

Stern, D. N. (2004). *The Present Moment in Psychotherapy and Everyday Life.* New York: W. W. Norton.

Stolorow, R. (2007). *Trauma and Human Existence: Autobiographical, Psychoanalytic, and Philosophical Reflections.* New York: Routledge.

Strachey, J. (1962). The term "Angst" and its English translation. *The Standard Edition of the Complete Psychological Works of Sigmund Freud, 3*: 116–117. London: Hogarth.

Sullivan, H. S. (1953). *The Interpersonal Theory of Psychiatry.* New York: W. W. Norton.

Summers, R., & Barber, J. (2010). *Psychodynamic Therapy: A Guide to Evidence-Based Practice.* New York: Guilford.

Symington, J., & Symington, N. (1996). *The Clinical Thinking of Wilfred Bion.* New York: Routledge.

Tangney, J. P., & Dearing, R. L. (2002). *Shame and Guilt.* New York: Guilford.

Tansey, M. J. (1994). Sexual attraction and phobic dread in the countertransference. *Psychoanalytic Dialogues, 4*: 139–152.

Thomason, K. (2018). *Naked: The Dark Side of Shame and Moral Life.* Oxford: Oxford University Press.

Tillman, J. G. (2006). When a patient commits suicide: An empirical study of psychoanalytic clinicians. *International Journal of Psychoanalysis, 87*: 159–177.

Tronick, E. (2007). *The Neurobehavioral and Social–Emotional Development of Infants and Children.* New York: W. W. Norton.

Van der Hart, O. (2016). Pierre Janet, Sigmund Freud, and dissociation of the personality: The first codification of a psychoanalytic depth psychology. In: E. Howell & S. Itzkowitz (Eds.), *The Dissociative Mind in Psychoanalysis: Understanding and Working With Trauma* (pp. 44–56). New York: Routledge.

Van der Hart, O., Nijenhuis, R. S., & Steele, K. (2006). *The Haunted Self: Structural Dissociation and the Treatment of Chronic Traumatization.* New York: W. W. Norton.

Wachtel, P. L. (2007). *Relational Theory and the Practice of Psychotherapy.* New York: Guilford.

Wallin, D. (2007). *Attachment in Psychotherapy.* New York: Guilford.

Wampold, B., & Imel, Z. (2015). *The Great Psychotherapy Debate: The Evidence for What Makes Psychotherapy Work.* New York: Routledge.

Welles, J. K., & Wrye, H. K. (1991). The maternal erotic countertransference. *International Journal of Psychoanalysis, 72*: 93–106.

Wilderson, F. (2020). *Afropessimism.* New York: W. W. Norton.

Winnicott, D. W. (1949). Hate in the counter-transference. *International Journal of Psychoanalysis, 30*: 69–74.

Winnicott, D. W. (1965). Communicating and not communicating leading to a study of certain opposites. In: *The Maturational Processes and the Facilitating Environment* (pp. 179–192). Madison, CT: International Universities Press.

Winnicott, D. W. (1974). Fear of breakdown. *International Review of Psycho-Analysis, 1*: 103–107.

Winnicott, D. W. (1992). *Through Pediatrics to Psychoanalysis: Collected Papers.* New York: Routledge.

World Health Organization (2021). Suicide data. https://who.int/teams/mental-health-and-substance-use/suicide-data (last accessed May 1, 2021).

Wurmser, L. (1977). *The Mask of Shame.* Lanham, MD: Jason Aronson.

Wurmser, L. (2003). The annihilating power of absoluteness: Superego analysis in the severe neuroses, especially in character perversion. *Psychoanalytic Psychology, 20*: 214–235.

Wurmser, L. (2012). Negative therapeutic reaction and the compulsion to disappoint the other. In: L. Wurmser & H. Jarass (Eds.), *Nothing Good Is Allowed to Stand: An Integrative View of the Negative Therapeutic Reaction* (pp. 27–56). New York: Routledge.

Wurmser, L. (2015). Primary shame, mortal wound and tragic circularity: Some new reflections on shame and shame conflicts. *International Journal of Psychoanalysis, 96*: 1615–1634.

Wurmser, L., & Jarass, H. (Eds.) (2008a). *Jealousy and Envy: New Views about Two Powerful Feelings.* New York: Analytic Press.

Wurmser, L., & Jarass, H. (2008b). Introduction. In: L. Wurmser & H. Jarass (Eds.), *Jealousy and Envy: New Views about Two Powerful Feelings* (pp. xi–xix). New York: Analytic Press.

Wurmser, L., & Jarass, H. (2008c). Pathological jealousy: The perversion of love. In: L. Wurmser & H. Jarass (Eds.), *Jealousy and Envy: New Views about Two Powerful Feelings* (pp. 1–23). New York: Analytic Press.

Zimmer, R. B. (2013). Arrogance and surprise in the psychoanalytic process. *Psychoanalytic Quarterly, 82*: 393–412.

Žižek, S. (1992). *Looking Awry: An Introduction to Jacques Lacan through Popular Culture.* Cambridge, MA: Massachusetts Institute of Technology Press.

# Index